The Ways of a Yorkshire Dale

For Julie and Sarah — my daughters

The Ways of a
Yorkshire Dale

by
Barry Cockcroft

Dalesman Books
1981

The Dalesman Publishing Company Ltd.,
Clapham, via Lancaster, LA2 8EB

First published by J.M. Dent & Sons Ltd., 1974
(as "Sunley's Daughter")

This first paperback edition 1981

ISBN: 0 85206 619 8

Also by Barry Cockcroft

Hannah in Yorkshire

Printed by Galava Printing Company Limited, Nelson, Lancashire

Contents

Photographs in the text are on pages 33-40, 57-64 and 81-88.

Acknowledgements

I owe much gratitude to the entirely admirable people who feature in this book for their friendship and co-operation; my sincere thanks are also extended to John Fairley, Mostafa Hammuri, Julie O'Hare, Graham Shrimpton, Paul Dunstan and to all the other members of the YTV team who helped to make the two televison documentaries on which a substantial part of this book is based; to Alan Harbour (who took the cover) and Brian Jeeves for their photography; to Mrs Ruth Fletcher of Glaisdale for allowing me to use passages from 'Queen of the Dales', the memoirs of the late George Harland; to Janice Robertson, who has edited both my books; and to Jackie, who waited.

East of the Cleveland Hills

To the east of the Cleveland Hills lies a land as strangely seductive as any in this island. It is watered by the river Esk, which wanders sinuously across the bracken moors and with a pewtered languor through villages which have changed remarkably little since the young Captain Cook walked towards immortality along its banks. He followed the Esk to Whitby, where it spills out into the North Sea.

This land is best entered through the looping branches of the great crippled chestnut tree in the grounds of Guisborough Priory, which once made the major oak of Sherwood Forest look like a promising youth; it concludes among the dragon's teeth of the ruined Abbey of Whitby. In between there are people whose lives Thomas Hardy might have described.

Eskdale and the rest of East Cleveland contain all the hypnotic beauty of the Western Dales, with purple garlanded hills plunging into quilted valleys and grouse moors that stretch like moonscapes into the far distance. But these Eastern fells stand aloof, their shoulders rubbed by a neighbour the others know nothing of. The sea.

Over the centuries, the people of the Esk have faced up to the pressures brought upon them by the sea, taken what they thought might help them in the defence of their heritage and thrown the residue back over the looming cliffs. Never have they allowed their links with the land to be severed, or the sharply drawn line between yeoman and seaman to become diffused. The land has always been the unchallenged source of life, and the use and possession of it remain paramount. Walk less than half a mile inland and you will find among the people a distaste for the sea which resembles the suspicion and hostility of opposed religions.

There is also a sharp difference in the personality of the people on each side of the Cleveland hills. The Clevelanders can be positively Sicilian in their attitudes, whereas the land to the west is a more gregarious place. Even the minerals under the two surfaces seem to reflect this dichotomy. The western soil yields lead, a pliant metal. In the east it changes to iron.

There is a studied indifference to the blandishments of the outside world that tends to be confirmed historically. It has never been necessary to go through the heart of East Cleveland to get to anywhere except East Cleveland. In fact, local historians say that the Reformation scarcely touched this land and the influence of the Roman Catholic Church appears to be far stronger here than in the Western Dales. Population movement has been minimal apart from migratory phases, which has led to a widespread and intricate pattern of light inbreeding. Everyone seems to be a cousin, many times removed, to everyone else.

Even in summer tourists are thin on the ground in these valleys. In winter an outsider is sometimes made to feel that it is a vague obscenity to bring a saloon car onto the twisting, changeless lanes. This is horse country, given over to hunting and shooting and a kind of rural life that disappeared elsewhere with the working horse. As far as the motor is concerned, only the Land Rover belongs.

The landscape of the Esk valley has altered little since the lanes and moorland bridle tracks were bustling with packhorse traffic and herds of cows, which had to be shod by roadside blacksmiths to prevent them being irreparably lamed on the long journey between market and port. Every mile by day carried at least one monk travelling between Rievaulx and Guisborough, or Rosedale and Whitby. At night they were replaced by less pious traffic, as smugglers stealthily hauled their silks and barrels of French brandy, hooves muffled.

The horse is still the best way to travel these roads and it remains the way of the Eskdalian when he is being true to his blood. Indeed, the stern spirit of all East Cleveland is symbolised by a horse, bred in these hills for countless generations and named after the slopes which guard the western approaches. The Cleveland Bay is said with some justification to be the finest breed of horse in the world.

It is certainly a horse for all seasons. You can hitch a Cleveland Bay to a glass coach, as the Queen does, or harness him to a plough; blaze a trail over the hedges and dry stone walls behind the hounds; enter him (after some genetical reshaping) for the Derby; or simply hack him from York to London. There is nothing a Shire horse or an Arab stallion can do which a Cleveland Bay cannot.

The catechism of the Cleveland Bay is repeated wherever you go. Since before the Middle Ages, this area has been famous for its skill in breeding 'clean-legged horses, traditionally bay in colour', which were infinitely adaptable to the transport and agricultural needs of the day. It is firmly believed that these horses were blood brothers to the Yorkshire gallowers or galloways, used for racing and reared on the same hills. The galloway was to become the mother of the most aristocratic horses in history. Every thoroughbred horse in the world is descended from seventy-eight foundation mares and three stallions brought from the east. More than seventy of these mares were galloways bred in North Yorkshire.

The late Sir Alfred Pease, a redoubtable champion of the

Cleveland Bay in his time, wrote that every Cleveland in the stud book could be traced back to the eighteenth-century racing sires. Even in those days the strain was kept pure from 'cart blood', but it was crossed with thoroughbreds to evolve the Yorkshire coach horse known at the time as the 'New Cleveland Bay', which hauled the carriages of the gentry all over Europe and farther afield during most of the nineteenth century. Sir Alfred wrote:

'During the height of the London season hundreds of pairs of these magnificent animals might be seen in Hyde Park every afternoon. Until 1884 they were included by the public at least, in the general term "Cleveland Bays".'

The date is significant. It was in that year that the Cleveland Bay Horse Society was founded and the first stud book published. Sir Alfred was among the upstanding body of men who drafted its first official pronouncement:

'We assert without fear of contradiction that the old type of Cleveland is the best and most economical animal on a farm; that it will do more work in any given period of time, consume less food, wear less shoe iron in either slow or fast work on the farm or on the road, than any other breed. The old type of Cleveland — deep and wide, capable of any kind of farm and road work, fast or slow, should stand about sixteen hands high. Back not too long, strong, with muscular loins. Shoulder sloping, deep and muscular. Quarters level, powerful, long and oval, the tail springing well from the quarters. Bone nine to ten and a half inches below the knee.'

The feats of the Cleveland have been lovingly recorded by the society for almost a century. As a pack-horse it could carry sixteen stones sixteen miles within the hour, at a trot. One prodigious animal apparently hauled seven hundred pounds sixty miles in twenty-four hours four times a week. 'Elephants and camels can be found to carry the weight, but how long would they take to do the four journeys?' the Society demanded triumphantly.

The coach horses of the last century owed much of their quality to the Cleveland. When John Macadam wrought his revolution on our roads, stage coaches were able to race the four hundred miles between London and Edinburgh in forty hours. Ten miles an hour! So amazing was this speed considered that the coaches were described as 'Flying Machines' and Lord Campbell wrote a cautionary word of advice:

'This swift travelling was considered dangerous as well as wonderful, and I was gravely advised to stay a day at York, as several passengers who had gone through without stopping died of apoplexy from the rapidity of the motion.'

But the best story of the Cleveland Bay is more recent, and says more than any other about the breed of Cleveland horse — and man.

A farmer called Arthur Bell worked his forty acres with a Cleveland. One day he was out ploughing when the Hunt went by in full cry. The horse promptly leapt out of the furrow and chased after them, plough and all. Mr Bell was more than equal to the occasion. He cut the traces, mounted the horse and stayed with the hounds right to the kill.

He was presented with the fox's brush.

Masters of Horse

A handful of men, and one woman, make stern and dedicated work of ensuring that the Cleveland Bay remains monarch of the Eskdale fells, feeling quite properly that the continuance and advancement of the breed should spring from the place where it evolved.

Look all over this island and you will not find men more rooted in the land, more sure that the ways and beliefs of their fathers, grandfathers and beyond are the right ones, so uncompromisingly countrymen with an unshakeable dislike of most things urban. Some of them appear to have been frozen in sepia and only recently released from the evocative camera of Frank Meadow Sutcliffe, the immortal recorder of life in North East Yorkshire a century ago. And these men wear the attitudes (and it would seem in some cases, the clothes) of their forefathers with the insularity and prickly pride of an age thought to have been totally lost, when the man of the house was head of a small empire and everyone around him his subject. To this day along the waters of the Esk, there are women and children who hold their husbands and fathers in genuine awe. They do what they are told unquestioningly, sometimes in fear. But they are also sure that it is only right and proper that the head of the house should receive the same respect that he gave to his father.

Men like this possess an aura, a kind of inner power which can be felt instantly by people to whom this way of life is something they have only heard or read about, people from the mainstream of today's life.

It is fascinating to see these two worlds meet, to witness the shock of recognition by the one that the other is from a different timescale. Anyone who tries to claim easy familiarity with these flinty men of the hills will be frozen into mute confusion. They are not afraid of speaking their minds, another lost principle which still flourishes in Eskdale. And the person who enjoys all the benefits of modern civilisation, prepared and shaped by amazing technology to be ready for the twenty-first century, is also the one who bends the knee in this slow collision. He is the one forced to adapt, to acknowledge that he has come face to face with a culture which has more purpose and strength than his own.

Do not assume, however, that this strength precludes all the joys of living. There is humour, poetry and song in the souls of these people which sweeten and temper the overall sternness, but they are not paraded for the benefit of casual observers.

Curiously enough, the two most uncompromising men in the ranks of the Cleveland Bay breeders and owners are poets and writers of considerable experience and some talent. Separately, America Jack Welford and Joe Sunley look as though they could frighten a rampant Cleveland stallion into fawning docility with one look — indeed, they frequently do — but together (and with the help of one particular woman) they could run an Eisteddfod. Both are chieftains of their clan, members of the ruling body of the Cleveland Bay Horse Society, vying with each other for the prizes in the Cleveland Bay classes of the local shows and for space in the Society's magazine to promote their verses. The extraordinary woman who complements them, Miss Ruth Kitching, matches their personalities with considerable flair.

But the two men are divided in several important ways. America Jack has a powerful physique, Joe is of slight build. Their original backgrounds differ because the Welfords have been wedded to one piece of land for countless generations, whilst Joe is from mining stock. Although a casual observer could be forgiven for failing to recognise it, a strong vein of humour runs through America whereas Joe, who smiles a lot more, is by and large a prophet of doom, the Cleveland Cassandra who believes the world is about to cut itself to pieces.

> Horses and Women he thinks them the same
> Plenty of Work, a lot less rein.

The world of America Jack Welford looks as though it will survive anything. For sure, it has resisted most of the assaults of science and progress up to now.

America Jack stands on his wind-whipped hill overlooking Runswick Bay in the old wapentake of Langbaurgh East and defies the second half of the twentieth century to advance an inch up the long cruel track to his bleak stone fortress of a farm.

This ironclad attitude is emphasised each year when his corn is ready for threshing. Grinding its way up the track, dragged by two tractors comes an enormous antique, a threshing machine the size of a single decker tram and twice as old, which halts by his stacks and proceeds to grumble, snarl and shake itself like a wet dinosaur. Threshing Day is not the event it used to be in the Dales, a festival attended by all the neighbours with barrels of home-made beer to wash away the corn dust, and a long evening of ballads and home killed pork to follow, but the memory lingers on at America's place. Six or seven of his own kind appear as if from nowhere like wraiths from the past, silent men with faces of old leather dressed in shapeless tweeds and fustians, who attend the machine's convulsions in a kind of agricultural High Mass. Little conversation passes between them as they go about their slow ritual but there is deep understanding and contentment floating about the air along with the blinding chaff.

America presides over the proceedings with all the geniality of an undertaker. He is an absolute authoritarian and his farm is his fief, although his abrupt manner conceals a genuine hospitality which becomes apparent once he has grown to accept you. He can be a frightening figure as he looms dourly into view, a hawkish man in his middle sixties with bristling eyebrows and deliberate gait. His mere presence adds another dimension to the atmosphere and the light seems to drop a F stop or so. Anger him, and you suffer the kind of fear you last felt in a headmaster's study.

But engage his friendship and he will invite you to hunt with him on the glistening back of one of his Cleveland Bays. And if something amusing happens you may be privileged to hear a ballad commemorating the occasion on your next visit, written and sung by America.

America Jack Welford takes his name from his isolated farm, America House, which stands between the hamlet of Newton Mulgrave and the sullen wastes of Borrowby Moor. It is marked clearly on the map of Yorkshire made by William Colling Hobson in 1844. The Welfords have proliferated for centuries in the area, so it is traditionally necessary to distinguish between them by using double-barrelled Christian names. The first wife of America's father, George, did not help this situation by having seventeen children. America himself has seven sons and two daughters.

There is no way of knowing how long a farm has stood on this spot or when the Welfords first came to scratch a living here. If they were the original tenants one feels it would have been fitting. It was built by the Turton family, who have always been powerful landowners in East Cleveland and still are, and an inscription in the weathered stone announces that it was rebuilt in 1851. Like unnumbered ancestors before him, America still pays his rent to the Turtons at Kildale Hall, which again demonstrates the amazing continuity of life in many of the Yorkshire Dales.

This otherwise unbroken chain snapped briefly shortly after the farm was rebuilt, when for unknown reasons the Welfords abandoned it. Legend says that the new tenants gave the place its present name. America says his father remembers them.

'Aye, they were called Harding and they were from America. I don't know what they were doing to come here but they couldn't have done so well in the end. They had to cut up the steps of the stairs and the window frames, to get some fuel for the fire I suppose. You can still see where they chopped the main beams out of the cow house. Some of them are still lying there. Anyway, before they came here the place had been called New Farm. We had it in those days but I don't know how many generations back, although my father's grandfather worked it. It came back to the Welfords in 1880 when my father took it over. It was lying derelict, you see, and the Turtons asked us to go back.'

As the Hardings beat a miserable retreat to goodness knows where (back to their roots, perhaps, as the New Frontier opened up in the West?), leaving behind them permanent memorials in a new name for the maps and some savaged timbers, George Welford laid the foundations of his prodigious family. The fading copperplate roll-call of names in the family Bible goes on endlessly ... Dan, Fred, Will, Hannah, Jane, Thomas, Kate, Page, Lily, George, Laura.... And when his first wife died he married Mary, America's mother, who gave him two more children. That made nineteen....

America remembers them all, except Page, 'He was burned to death as a child, right here at this fireside. Seems they went out to milk and his nightgown caught fire. My father never allowed us to burn rags on the fire from that day on—I reckon the smell of 'em reminded him.

'Mind, I don't remember much of Dan, the eldest, either. He emigrated to Canada—or was it Australia?—when I was about five or six. I can still remember him coming to me to say farewell. It was the last time I saw him.'

How in those penurious times George Welford managed to raise nineteen children on his one hundred and seventy-four unyielding acres (for even proud America will admit that it is not good farming land) is a secret locked away in the mists that regularly roll down from the high moor to shroud the barns and outbuildings. America steadfastly refused to talk about his young life (and only a foolhardy man would persist), which indicates that the memory could be painful. Certainly, other farming families in the same area endured a kind of poverty which is difficult to comprehend these days. America concedes that there was not too much money to spare, that sometimes they barely scraped through and such things as presents at Christmas were unheard of. It is popularly believed that farmers never go hungry because they grow food but there were times on other farms when even the last dozen eggs had to go to market and not into the pan, and father's skill with a rabbit snare was the only thing to bring meat to the table.

America will tell you about walking miles to school in his clogs and cord britches, scratching away at his slate in the infant school and being afraid of policemen. But not much else about his childhood. Mary Welford was a staunch Catholic and on Sundays would walk her children four miles to Mass, or go down with a horse and cart which would be hitched up outside the local pub. Her husband was sixty-five when he fathered America, and the new son of the house inherited two qualities from his sire: an indomitable character and a lifelong passion for the Cleveland Bay horse. George Welford, like

14

his father before him, was a member of the Society, which was formed in the 1880s, and nursed a ferocious loyalty for the breed. His association with the Society ended in explosive resignation the day the King of England innocently meddled in its affairs.

Horse breeders often become fanatical about one particular breed of horse but the members of the Cleveland Bay Society nurse a positive obsession about the purity of their horseflesh. They are particularly scathing about the coach horse breed, which is part Cleveland Bay and part blood, which adds a touch of swagger. Certain men (according to the diehards) fall prey to this false glamour and such a man was King George the Fifth of England, Defender of the Faith but not that of the Cleveland Bay. He actually ran a stud of the detested coach horses. In his day most shows did not have separate competitions for the Cleveland Bay and they were forced to enter the same class as the coach horse. Noble though the Cleveland Bay was it rarely won anything against the born actors mincing around the same ring.

King George owned a famous stallion called Tantalus which must have created agonies in the Society by taking just about every prize on offer. And in 1921, with the best of motives, he offered Tantalus to the Cleveland Bay Society in the touching belief that it would improve the breed. There is one man today who says that he would have given a hundred guineas to be present in the room when this news was announced to those granite-jawed men. In a row unprecedented in the Cleveland Hills for a century, the Society split fairly down the middle: those who said that it was impossible, as loyal subjects, to look a royal gift horse in the mouth despite the pain, and those Cromwellians who urged that the 'mongrel' should be whipped all the way back to Windsor. The Royalists won, and reluctantly placed the name of Tantalus in their cherished official pedigree stud book. The rest tore up their membership cards and left the Society in a black rage.

One of those who never returned was George Welford. He declared he was through with the Society for ever and he was a man who did not lightly go back on his word.

'He wouldn't even allow a coach horse on this farm,' says his son, in some awe.

Rows have always been part of the fabric of the Society's history, which is inevitable when you consider the baronial personalities involved. There had been a similar conflict in 1888, which was won by the purists, when a group of members tried to get a tainted animal into the stud book. The losers resigned to form the Yorkshire Coach Horse Society. It is more than probable that these rows were accompanied by violence, in the best Queensbury tradition. Men have always been real men in the Cleveland Bay Society and the last recorded bout of fisticuffs at a meeting was only ten years ago. Two prominent members hurled abuse at each other over some matter involving a gelding before stepping outside to settle the issue in a way which would doubtless have earned a nod of approval from their ancestors. Indeed, one very senior member at this meeting was clearly pleased at the turn of events because it brought back so many vivid memories.

'This is quite like old times,' he declared happily. 'We rarely had a meeting in the old days without someone starting a fight.'

Incidentally, as things turned out, the dreaded Tantalus was not allowed to stain the stud book indelibly. He was permitted to sire a few foals — chestnuts, would you believe? — and then craftily sold off to Canada after three years. But an ocean away still was not far enough for America's father. And today according to Ruth Kitching, who practically carries the entire stud book in her head, there 'isn't a smell of Tantalus to be found'. Even now, the deadliest insult you can level against a dedicated Cleveland Bay man is to suggest that the parentage of *his* stallion is suspect. There is only one way to redress that kind of situation in these hills, a reaction which comes as naturally to America Welford as any other. In fact, he once came close to combat with the Professor of Agriculture at Leeds University, a story which Ruth Kitching tells with relish.

'One day at my farm I had a very egg-headed group on a visit. I belonged to a group called the Yorkshire Agricultural Adventurers which was linked to Leeds University, and they had asked to come over and look at the grass. There were about twenty students led by Professor McGregor, a very nice chap, and it was a lovely summer evening. They'd seen the cows and the grass and the sheep and had come down to the yard and there was America, much younger then, of course, holding a very nice Cleveland Bay stallion which he'd brought to see if I wanted any of my mares covering. He was horrified to see all my visitors, being a shy man, but he urged me to take advantage of the stallion because he thought it the best the Dale had seen for years. I was a bit doubtful, you see, because I didn't particularly want any foals at the time since trade was poor. At this moment dear old Professor McGregor obviously decided to have a bit of fun with America because it's pretty certain he knew that to suggest to a Cleveland man that his horse might have a bit of blood in him was to invite trouble. He looked at America sideways, examined the animal and said: "Very nice...a nice sort of horse... most interesting. But I had always imagined they were a little stronger....I am surprised. Do you think it possible that your horse has a little alien blood in him?"

'It really was very naughty of him, of course, and when the meaning of all this havering dawned on America he drew himself up to his full height, transfixed him with a glare and announced: "If you're saying my horse has thoroughbred blood in him I shall knock you down!"

'I think he was going to do just that when the Professor said:

16

"Nothing so violent I hope. Perhaps one of my companions will deputise for me." Anyway, it was smoothed over and we all went in for a cup of tea.'

In these days, mares are brought to the stallion for covering but there was once a time when it was arranged the other way around. Stallions would go on tour, touting for business like a tinker. Their itinerary would be locally advertised: 'Bay Devil, property of Mr Reuben Raw, will stand (health permitting) at the Mitre Inn, Glaisdale, at noon for two hours. Afterwards at Mr J. Atkinson's farm at Egton until four of the clock....' A popular price was a guinea for covering and a guinea when the mare was proved in foal. The entry of a prize stallion at the head of a Dale always sent a ripple of excitement surging ahead, as the mares in the fields picked up his scent and began to rear and gallop furiously around, filling the air with a piercing welcome. Anyone who has seen a stallion respond to these siren calls will realise how powerful a man had to be to control him and keep him moving on to his appointed assignations.

America is such a man and he recalls many such tours, when man and horse had to be very fit. 'Sometimes we'd both be soaked to the skin before we were half way through but a good stallion would manage six or seven mares in a day. Maybe we'd get two or three in foal.' In the season, a prime stallion would cover a hundred mares and several hundred miles. America is a renowned stallion handler and the keeper of the Cleveland Bay Society's precious beast, Mulgrave.

A procession of horseboxes lurches unsteadily up to his mellow stone stables for America to superintend the union impassively. However rampant the stallion may feel, there is no doubt whatsoever about who is master. The power of this man is almost tangible. He just talks to the animal in a strange language and it obeys. The old price paid by owners of mares has risen by around thirty times or more in some cases.

America has also broken more horses than more urban folk have seen. Soon after leaving school at the age of fourteen he relished the chance of subduing a good young horse and used to saddle two or three a year. His father, who ran six or seven Clevelands when times were favourable, was a regular follower of the Glaisdale Hunt. America has continued the tradition, still riding today with a remarkable fluency, maintaining an erect back not often seen now. He owns a prize mare, Bay Lass, a yearling filly plus another mare and breeds some delightful foals, which he has sold in the past to several countries, including America. One even made the journey from that severe hill to the elegant atmosphere of the Royal Mews, to help pull the Queen's coaches. America is reputed to make more money than most from his skill at breeding Clevelands, although he will tell you that he 'loses less' than the others. Certainly, his lifelong enthusiasm for the breed has been a costly act of faith because there had been no profit in horses for a generation, until six or seven years ago. Now the price for a top class Cleveland can spiral higher than £700.

America recalls selling Clevelands in the 'thirties and 'forties for as little as thirty or forty pounds which today would bring a gallop of cheque books up his hill.

At the time he was glad to get anything because life for him as a young man was not at all easy. He married an ironstone miner's daughter from Scaling whose dark-eyed beauty as a young girl is still remembered in East Cleveland, and his father was still in command when he brought his bride up to the cold comfort of America House. The year was 1928, and George Welford did not retire until a few years before his death in 1937 at the age of eighty-four. Phyllis, the young Mrs Welford, was plunged immediately into the back-breaking work of the farm, helping to make butter and curds for market, milking and doing countless other tasks. Of course, there was no electricity—just oil lamps—and no water on tap or other luxuries. The water had to be carried in pails from a trough by the spring at the top of the field in front of the house. And then the children began to arrive, starting with George in 1931. Over the next twenty years he was followed by Bertha, Hilda, Dennis, John, Edgar, Cyril, Alan and Brian. Seven sons and two daughters naturally had a telling effect on the family resources. But there was the compensation of many hands to do the work as they grew up, and in those days the children of the Yorkshire Dales had their appointed tasks before they went to school in the morning, and on their return.

His father's longevity and reluctance to retire until he was nearly eighty at least ensured that America inherited the farm. Tradition-ally, the eldest son of a Dales farmer takes over and the others are obliged to go. But all America's stepbrothers had tired of waiting and had scattered long before. Significantly, only one became a farmer, but the others were unable to break completely with the land and became woodmen and gamekeepers. Only Thomas, better known as Tot, and Will were still living in 1974.

America had yearned for his own farm since childhood. No other dreams had entered his young head. He was daily confronted with the romantic lure of the sea. The broad sweep of Runswick Bay seems to lap up to the farm's lower fields, although it is a good two miles away. But America's eye was never beguiled by the seascape under his nose, which when he was a lad, often rivalled a painting by Whistler, full of tall masted clippers with reflecting sails.

'No, I never had no use for the sea,' he says. 'It has no appeal for me at all.'

This low opinion of the sea appears to be universally shared by all the farm people of East Yorkshire. It can't be ploughed, doesn't support sheep or carry horses so what use is it? And the land rises from the shore to a hundred feet in places, the highest cliffs in

England, as if it shares this distaste and places its precious fields well out of reach of the water's grasp.

When America finally succeeded to the farm on his father's death he had no desire to change its basic ways and it remains to this day a monument to tradition. The interior of his house is much as it was in his father's day, crammed with stout and mellow old furniture, with Mrs Welford scurrying around with the same baking trays. The hearth always seems to be full of rising dough and the tables spread with fresh-baked bread, scones and cakes — and delicious they are, too. The dark brown corners of his barns and outbuildings are redolent with the smell of old leather and new corn, crowded with the agricultural bric-à-brac of generations which hang from the beams and hooks and lean against the cobwebbed walls.

Many of his farming ways remain exactly the same, too. To climb the hill to America House on sheep-branding day, for instance, is like stepping back at least half a century in time. In the morning the sheep appear out of the clammy mists on the lip of the high moor, urged on by America from horseback. As the dogs drive them down to the pens two of his sons, George and Edgar, stoke a brazier to a fierce heat until the branding iron glows red.

Then the tall and immensely strong George starts a day long wrestling match. Each struggling sheep is seized with one hand and dragged between his knees, whilst the other hand presses home the branding iron, the muscles of his forearm bulging with the effort. Often the sheep's horn catches fire as the iron bites into it, and the air fills with the bitter smell. Each horn is branded with the initials G.W. — George Welford — which means the iron is the best part of a hundred years old. The young George, eldest son, seems set to inherit the farm for he lives at home and appears to have few interests outside agriculture. He is an expert with Swaledale sheep and runs a sizeable flock, although his father refuses to say how many beyond 'between a hundred and a thousand'. Beef cattle are also raised on the farm, along with a bewildering array of minor animals and birds, such as guinea fowl, geese and goats.

Life at America House is not as dour as it may appear to a casual visitor. Even in the old days there was time for a little sport, although — as you might imagine — even the pleasure on America's domain has changed not one whit down the years. There is still a set of horseshoes around the place, for America was a skilled quoits player in his younger days, but the most fun is centred round the merrils board. Before the last war, every farm played merrils and a board was traditionally carved into the wooden top of the fodder bin in the stable. It is an exceedingly complicated game to an outsider, something like a cross between draughts and chess. The pieces are round and flat pegs, always fashioned by hand, which are stuck into holes in the board and the game gets pretty tense in the decisive stages. A game between experts lasts about ten minutes and it is said that in the old days if you saw the oil lamps in any stable in East Cleveland burning late at night it would mean that a session of merrils was under way. Almost exactly the same game is played by the peasants of Turkey, although no one has been able to establish any connection.

If you turn over America's merril board you can try your hand at another antiquated game — fox and goose. This side looks more like a solitaire board and the goose had a flock of thirteen pegs whilst the fox only has one. The object of the fox is to get behind the geese and that of the geese to pin down the fox. This game is just as confusing as merrils, and just as absorbing to America and his sons.

The few concessions that America has made to the space age have been eminently sensible and nothing has been done to damage the unique ecology of his farm. The water is now piped to the house and in 1956 he seized upon an opportunity offered in all innocence by the Yorkshire Electricity Board to bring power to farms for the flat rate of £186. The Board's engineers must have been more than dismayed when America applied. They had to erect poles and lines all the way from Ellerby, which is two and a half miles away as the seagull flies!

But no telephone has been installed — that would be going too far and America knows it. Yet he enjoys using the telephone as an instrument for practical joking. He will go down to the village to 'phone and many people have picked up their receiver to hear a voice saying: 'Will you take a call from America?' which generally causes a certain amount of panic. America's sense of humour is becoming a legend in the surrounding valleys. For instance, when the Cleveland Society made a film with the help of local photographer and chemist John Tindale, the final shot was of Ruth Kitching's stable door closing to reveal a carefully constructed sign saying 'Cleveland Bay Horse Society: The End'. The rehearsal worked perfectly, and the 'crew' went into Ruth's house for a cup of tea before the take. Then the super 8 mm camera rolled, the horse went into the stable like clockwork, the door closed and the lens zoomed in on 'The End' — but there was an extra garnish on the sign. A tin of corned beef!

Perhaps the most oft-repeated tale about America concerned the day he was driving a flock of fifty hungry sheep, fresh from the inhospitable moor, along a village road. Some poor old lady had failed to shut her garden gate and the sheep rushed straight in.

'There wasn't a plant left inside two minutes and the owd lady came out spitting blood,' recalls America. 'I just stood there looking gormless and said it were nowt to do wi' me because they weren't my sheep but she said that someone would have to pay. I told her to apply to the local Midland bank manager, Eddie Cummin, because he owned 'em and would doubtless pay up. She was most suspicious about this and later asked her milkman if he thought this would be true. Now it happened that her milkman was my cousin's son, and he was a bit quick, like. He said: "Was it a great big daft looking bugger, a bit gawky like?" "Aye that's 'im to a tee," she said. "Well then, that's Eddie Cummin's man," he said, which wasn't far from the truth because Eddie owned half the stock round here—well, we all had loans from him.'

Mr Cummin, who sadly died in 1971, was a staunch friend of the Cleveland Bay men and treasurer of their Society, and was probably as quick to understand the situation when the lady came to berate him.

America continues to wield his deadpan humour with devastating effect as he mellows into pensionable age, with life for the hill farmer much more comfortable and time to spare for leisure. His deep knowledge of the Cleveland breed has horse show secretaries competing for his services as a judge and he is clearly one of the best known personalities east of the Cleveland Hills. One feels that as long as this great big, marvellous gawky bugger continues to loom large over these fells, their heritage is quite safe.

To be perfectly frank, Miss Ruth Kitching really should not be rubbing girths with the likes of America Jack Welford, Joe Sunley and the other masters of horse. Her background is totally alien to theirs, her accent cuts across their Eskdalian *patois* like the Royal Yacht steaming through a herring fleet and, what is more, she is a woman!

But Ruth Kitching, barrister at law, has been fully accepted into the strange masonry of the Cleveland Bay men. So much so that she appears to come close to running the Society at times, although it would not be wise to venture this opinion in front of the other officers of the Society's council. Indeed, when one outsider was allowed to attend a council meeting one evening and wittily observed that the others looked like Kitching utensils he practically had to flee the room to escape the wrath of the men.

She won her unique place in this patrician group in the only possible way—the exercising of an indomitable spirit and half a lifetime of dedication to the breed. Ruth, in fact, is a member of a tiny and exclusive band who saved the Cleveland Bay from possible extinction some years ago. Her story is truly remarkable and demonstrates above all how strong the call of the land runs in the blood of the moors people. A deal of effort and much money was invested to try and purge this call from the Kitching line, but happily failed.

Ruth was born into an upper-middle-class family in Pickering and into a life cushioned by elegance, servants and a private income. She never had to boil an egg or sew on a button until she was twenty-one. The family home, Low Hall, is now the Forest and Vale Hotel in the centre of Pickering. Nevertheless, the Kitchings were irrevocably rooted in the land.

'My great-grandfather was a farmer and so was his great-grandfather I imagine. The Kitchings came to Pickering from Great Ayton, where there are still a lot of Kitchings, in 1745 and bought seven acres of land and a house for fifteen pounds ten shillings. The house is still standing. We must have done very well, for in the middle of the last century my grandfather, Robert, was put to the law and became a solicitor — his firm is still going strong. My father and his brother also became solicitors, but my father always wanted a farm. Eventually he acquired several farms in the Pickering area and lost a great deal of money on them. He finished up on a farm which he didn't even own, which was by chance a place dedicated to the Cleveland Bay. Father bred a lot of horses.'

Ruth, born in 1911, was fortunate in that the Kitchings believed in educating their women. An aunt was one of the first women doctors and her mother, who came from a wealthy shipping family in Whitby, was educated at Bedford College, London, and in Germany. She was an accomplished pianist. In fact, Ruth and her sisters became the fourth generation of well educated women and in her case it was expensive, for at the age of nine she went to a superior girls' boarding school in Scotland where she stayed until she entered Newnham College, Cambridge, in 1928.

All this sophistication could not diminish Ruth's passion for the land, which was shared by her elder sister Joan, who was allowed to go to the Studley Agricultural College for Ladies in Warwickshire to prepare her to take over a family farm.

'Then I came home from school and announced that I wanted to become a farmer too. I can picture the scene now, as we all perched round the sitting-room fire. My parents said with some anguish that one farmer was all the family could stand, because farming was in a pretty bad way at that time. Then I said I would be a vet, and they said certainly not. So my third wish was to be a lawyer, which horrified my mother because she thought it would be terribly dull, but rather tickled my father.'

So in the middle 'thirties, Ruth Kitching was duly called to the Inner Temple, and admitted to the bar whilst her sister was taught the more basic arts of making butter and cheese (which she practises to this day). She was in Chancery Chambers for a year and then studied common law before entering the Chambers of Geoffrey Wrangham, now Mr Justice Wrangham, in Bradford as a practising barrister.

Before moving back North, Ruth and a younger sister, Margaret, had lived a splendid life in London. They each had a private income of around £250, shared a desirable flat in Bayswater which cost two pounds a week and was cleaned by a woman for a shilling a day, and enjoyed life to the full. Ruth also supplemented her income, which was lavish for those days, by accepting a remarkable part-time job, secured for her by Newnham College. A worried Duke and Duchess had applied to the college for the name of a suitable young lady living in London, to assist with the final polishing of their wayward young daughter. She had refused point blank to go to finishing school in Paris and they were most anxious to instil a little culture into her life.

'For the enormous sum of three pounds a week, all I had to do was go round to their place in the mornings and take their daughter, who shall remain nameless, round museums and art galleries and the like. It was all rather splendid, but I was severely reprimanded by them once. I took her on a bus for the first time in her life and her parents were horrified when they found out. They considered travelling on buses most unhygienic and we almost had to take a bath there and then. Her Ladyship said that in future, if we couldn't get a taxi, we must telephone and a car would be sent round immediately.'

As a Bradford barrister, Ruth was just beginning to make her name on the Northern circuit and was earning a very healthy five or six hundred pounds a year when the last war broke out. She promptly left to join the Land Army.

'I needn't have gone, of course, and my clerk was astonished and furious. But I was a strong, countryminded female and there were plenty of elderly gentlemen around to look after legal matters.

'I was sent out to a big arable farm near Scarborough and I learned to milk cows by hand, which was a hellishly painful performance for both me and the cows. But we had a very understanding cowman who used to milk eight cows whilst I tortured the milk out of one. I used to mow thistles and do every job that came to hand — and enjoyed it. I was paid twelve shillings and sixpence a week after stoppages and I've never been so well off in my life. In fact, it was the only time I've never had an overdraft. We worked long hours, there was only one shop nearby and I had a job to spend a shilling a week. But we earned our money. I remember we had to catch the eight o'clock train with the milk, running smartly down to the station with three churns mounted on a trolley.'

Plunged though she was into the anonymous life of a rankless land-girl on an isolated farm, Ruth Kitching nevertheless managed to raise a wartime furore which reverberated through the Army High Command. The Kitchings had patriotically given over their splendid home in Pickering, with its beautiful gardens, generous stables, and mellow enclosing walls, to the military for a sergeants' mess. Some of the rooms, including the cellar, had been placed strictly out of bounds. As an extra precaution the cellar door had been barred and securely locked, but the sergeants smashed down the door and drank what remained of the Kitchings' bins of well bred wine. What the sergeants made of 1815 port, Tokay wine and other well set-up vintages is not recorded, but the port must have been very watery. Nevertheless the hand-made bottles with the seal and stamp were very rare and they had been smashed or stolen. When she heard of this desecration. Ruth was beside herself with rage.

'I might have taken a kinder view these days but I was young and brash and I thought this was bloody. So I sat down and wrote one of my Number One letters, not to the senior sergeant but to the G.O.C. Northern Command. Now it seems I should have just addressed the letter to G.O.C. Northern Command, Great Britain, because his exact location was a deadly secret. But you have to understand that in the country everybody knows everything and I know perfectly well where he hung out so I addressed it to Brompton Hall, Scarborough, Yorkshire. It never occurred to me that I shouldn't know.

'About two days after I sent the letter I was quietly hoeing turnips when chaps in uniform wearing mysterious badges—they were from M.I. something-or-other—descended on me. I thought they'd come about the cellar break-in and I was going on about it being an outrageous thing to happen in a free country, when they brushed all that aside and demanded how I came to know that the G.O.C. was at Brompton Hall. As it happened, the cowman was the first to tell me and I wasn't going to implicate him, so these chaps got very narked indeed. Eventually, they even held a court of inquiry to go into both matters but they couldn't do anything to me because it was obvious I wasn't an enemy agent. The poor G.O.C. probably had to change his lodgings. Anyway, they compensated me with two dozen bottles of the Lancers' best port, which wasn't very good as it happens.'

Even before the war ended, Ruth had decided not to go back to her law practice. 'I fully intended to return when I left my chambers at Bradford but then I realised I had to have a farm of my own.'

There were no parents to strangle the persistent call of the land this time and she took Fryup Hall, a couple of miles outside Lealholm, one of the loveliest villages embraced by the Esk. She was thirty-two and the year was 1944. What the local Eskdalians made of this rugged young woman with unusual ideas about farming, who spoke like a lady from the big house, enlivens the imagination. But they recognised her instantly as one of their own, and welcomed her. One of her neighbours, Mrs Frank Raw, became very concerned about a maiden lady living alone. She instructed Ruth to hang a white towel out of her bedroom window if she ever got into trouble or needed help, and she would send a man over instantly. There were no telephones in the dale then, and only two cars.

Ruth's farm was 'clean and poor' with two hundred and twenty acres of indifferent grass, but she wanted to found a pedigree herd. Her choice fell on Ayrshires, a breed completely unknown in the Dale, which caused much muttering and shaking of silvery heads in the other byres. Doom and disaster were prophesied for the Ayrshires but Ruth, with the help of her right hand, George Nelson, who was hired when she took over the farm and is still with her, built up a fine dairy herd and a flock of sixty ewes. Within a few years farms all over the Dale were milking Ayrshires.

She was also an experienced horsewoman, which did much to help her image in the Dale. There were no tractors then and most dwellings kept horses saddled all day in the stable like bicycles in a shed. Family transport was either a gig or a trap.

The new neighbour ran her farm with three draught horses, and one of these happened to be a bad tempered but very fine Cleveland Bay mare. The elders of the Cleveland Bay Horse Society spotted this quickly and immediately opened their doors, if not their hearts to her.

'In those days, anyone with a decent mare was allowed to join the council,' says Ruth, modestly.

What really happened, of course, was that her highly-trained mind brought many advantages to the Society, and her life-long expertise in the fine art of breeding horses, which is like a game of chess with genes, eventually proved vital in saving the breed. She launched and still edits the surprisingly literary Society magazine which is always teeming with humour and home-bred poetry, and she secured the position of assistant honorary secretary to the Society.

In 1962, Ruth decided 'to retire' and sold Fryup Hall, which she had bought in 1949. 'Altogether, I'd had twenty glorious years farming and I was over fifty, had a bad back and was very tired.' Retirement is a laughably inaccurate description of her activities from then on. She kept sixty acres of her land, fifty of her old ewes, built a stone bungalow and founded the Fryup Stud with the old mare, its three-year-old daughter...and a small colt called Chapman.

'I'd bought Chapman in 1960 not because I wanted him but because he was an outcross. You see, Clevelands are a very small and inbred strain but by a series of curious accidents Chapman wasn't closely related to the main stud horses. He was owned by a retired miner who probably wouldn't have been able to afford to keep a stallion and his mother was so old she probably wouldn't foal again. So I tried to persuade the top breeders to buy him, but they said he was too small and refused. Now I've always found pedigrees very easy to remember and I rather see horses in terms of how they are bred. I knew he must be bought and I got myself into quite a state about it so in the end I had no alternative but to buy him myself, although I'd got a colt foal off my old mare that year.'

It proved to be the most important decision for decades for the Cleveland Bay breed. Within two years, Chapman was the only outcross Cleveland stallion in the country, to the best of anyone's knowledge, and he then became even more important when the number of proven stallions in Britain was reduced by sales abroad.

'I think it true to say we were down to three, possibly four mature Cleveland stallions in this entire hemisphere. One of those was very old and related to just about everything and one may have been cut.

This was terribly bad management on the Society's part and I was as much to blame as anybody else. There were odd two year-olds knocking about but the Cleveland was in very real danger of becoming extinct and Chapman became a very valuable horse indeed to our breed, despite his stature.'

Chapman's progeny are still being born for he remains the star of the Fryup Stud, probably the best stallion around for certain lines. Ruth has the courage to run two stallions in her stud, which other Society members consider about as safe as sunbathing in the Sinai. She keeps them so far apart that they cannot see, hear or smell each other — but they know, and they show it. Her dedication allows no room for fear, however, and she has suffered physically because of her association with Clevelands. A horse backheeled her face at the Royal Show in 1967 breaking her jaw in two places and leaving a scar.

She has, indeed, sacrificed a great deal to take her place, shoulder-to-shoulder with the top men breeders who by and large believe that a woman is out of her depth when she steps out of her kitchen. She allows herself this modest boast: 'I am one of them in the sense that I farmed like them and I sweated like they sweated.' She also wins many of the top prizes for her horses, including awards at the Royal Show, which more than helps to kill any latent misogyny.

Ruth Kitching was a talented female barrister when such beings were much rarer than female farmers and it is more than possible that she would have risen along with Miss Rose Heilbron (or even preceded her) to legal glory. She rejected this, and all her suitors, for the simple but glorious rewards that the land gives to those who place it above all else.

Joe Sunley is built from the ironstone which is father mined with a great bitterness. There are no compromises in life for this small and slightly stopped man with hair so gleaming white that it stands like a heliograph when he is half a mile down his fields. Joe has a charisma which radiates with even greater strength. He deliberates every point with the gravity of a high court judge and he rules his farm at Girrick, down a narrow lane off the road between Guisborough and Whitby, without making many concessions to what most people accept as a normal lifestyle.

Joe's mother and father brought up five sons and two daughters at 195 Westgate, Guisborough. His father was a time-serving blacksmith but was obliged to give up this dignified trade and go into the iron ore mines which proliferated round the Guisborough area to earn the larger rewards dangled by the pit masters. His hatred of this work is clear in the ringing declaration he issued to his sons:

'I will take an axe and chop off your hands rather than let any of you go down a pit.'

None of them ever did.

The iron ore mines are all closed now, leaving behind the painful memory and a range of conical shale tips. One of the largest sticks out like a boil on the bottom of the otherwise beautiful vista from Joe's farm. Like America Welford's land a little farther south, Joe's fields appear to fall into the creamy embrace of the sea.

Sunley senior was a man of principle. He did not take the quickest way out of his misery like so many of his fellow miners, who spent a substantial proportion of their wages drowning their sorrows every week. Indeed, he was never known to get drunk. He insisted that his family wore leather boots, not clogs like all the others, and three-quarters of his money was spent on food.

'My father believed very strongly in us being shod with leather and keeping our bellies full,' says Joe. 'He had two sayings: "If your boots and hair are clean, you're half dressed" and "Back will trust, but belly won't".'

Life was still harsh for the Sunleys, particularly for the young Joe who caught diphtheria. It left a permanent mark on him.

'I was in a sanatorium for six months and I was left very weak. So to strengthen my legs I was sent to a school two miles away and I had to walk there and back every day. These days parents would be crying for a bus but mine were just the opposite and I think they were right.'

This kind of philosophy endures almost undiminished to this day at Joe's farm. The way of life there is probably unique in this country for its remorseless work cycle—up at 6 a.m. bring in the cows, milk by hand for three hours, swill out the byres and clean up the yard; have breakfast of cereal, hot milk, crackers, bread and tea. Then take out the cows, stack the bales of hay in the barn, manhandle the churns to the top of the road for collection, cut the grass, harvest the corn, play midwife to a pregnant cow; break for lunch at around 3.30 p.m., back out again to feed the horses, mend the fences, hack down the thistles, and work on until the cows come home again for another three hours of hauling away at their udders. Every day for sixteen hours, until nine at night and sometimes beyond. One hundred and twenty-six man (and woman) hours per week are spent milking, a job which could be done mechanically and in a fraction of the time if Joe had agreed to the intrusion of electricity.

If work is good for the soul, then Joe, his wife, Connie, and daughter Mary, are angels for sure.

But for Joe these hours are perfectly normal—he has always worked them, by and large. As a lad he rose at six, weakling or not, and ran to Guisborough railway station to pick up a bundle of newspapers which he then delivered round the town before going to school. The newsagent, a Mr Gill, was also a barber and the job, which paid two shillings and sixpence a week, also embraced the duties of lather-boy.

'We always worked until nine at night on Saturdays. There were four chairs and Mr Gill charged fourpence for a haircut and twopence for a shave. He could shave 'em as fast as I could lather 'em. Every Saturday night without fail just as the clock was striking nine and we were supposed to be shutting up shop a fishmonger would come in for a shave. I think he must have lived on fish that was going off because the stench from him was always horrible. He used to sit back in the chair and open his mouth wide, and I longed to get the biggest brush of lather I could and jam it in.'

When he left school he went to work in a bakery, greasing tins and weighing up, starting once again at 6 a.m. and working a twelve-hour day. His pay was three shillings a week and he was allowed to keep threepence for himself. At the age of fourteen, ready for man's work, he was apprenticed as a fitter and turner at the local foundry for six shillings a week, with a shilling rise every six months.

Joe and his family did not go to church with the rest of the crowd because his mother was a 'bit of a rebel' when it came to religion. 'She'd been tanned as a girl for not curtsying to the parson and this incident did not enamour her of the church,' says Joe. 'So I went to the Salvation Army because it was reckoned they did a bit of good. But when General Booth died and there was a big row over the million pounds he had collected from pennies on the drum I became a choirboy at the Parish Church. My pal was in the choir so I applied for an audition, with my parents' permission, and was accepted.'

Joe's romance with the established church did not, however, survive what he calls a 'broken promise'. Apparently the parson stopped the choir trips during the First World War, which led to a deputation asking for a resumption of this much coveted annual treat.

'He said there would be the best trip there had ever been when the war was over but it never happened.'

Joe is still a religious rebel, adhering to a set of beliefs which are exceedingly harsh when compared to the accepted norm. He is not liked for these views in some quarters of East Cleveland society but he never flinches from criticism. He says he is not religious in the formal sense, just lives 'by the Bible'. But for around two decades he has generally followed the dictum of the Jehovah's Witnesses sect, which is only for disciplinarians. Birthdays are not celebrated because the only two birthdays mentioned in the Bible were those of evil men. Christmas is not kept because the word from the Watchtower says Christ was born almost three months before December 25th. He believes the world will end in 1975 when all wickedness will be wiped out.

Yet there was once a time for Joe when life was sweet and whole-some and he was not so troubled by the sinfulness of men . . . when Connie walked into his life with a packet of sandwiches. She was seventeen then and a lass who would turn any young man's head as she walked along Applegarth, the Sunday afternoon parade ground for the young people of Guisborough. Connie had a friend who used to take tea to her father at the foundry, so she went with her one day and met Joe, who was then twenty-one and no longer a raw apprentice. They walked Applegarth together, and then the winding lanes to Connie's home three miles out of town. They became so wrapped up in each other that their walks went on for sixteen miles and more on those blissful Sundays of their youth.

Alas, their dreams of marriage and a home together were shattered by a double blow. Joe's father was invalided out of the mines with bronchitis and Joe, the eldest son, had to shoulder the responsibility of being the family's main breadwinner. And Connie's father died at the age of forty-nine. The Saturday following the funeral Connie, an only child, and her mother were obliged to get out of their house. Mother took a position as housekeeper and Connie went into service, working twelve hours a day for four shillings and sixpence a week.

For seven long years they courted, and walked, and waited. But instead of getting better, things got worse. Joe's mother died, and in 1931 he was made redundant. Two years later he was still out of work — and the unemployed received the dole for only the first six months in those black days of the Depression.

'By then I was twenty-eight you see, and I decided it was time to do something about getting married. So I had a talk with my father and he agreed that I had my own life to lead. Although I had no job I was turning my hand to anything that came along, growing food on two allotments, putting windows in for twice the price of the glass, anything. We went house hunting but no one would let me one as I was out of work. Then I met a man who had been foreman joiner at the place where I'd been employed. He'd set up on his own, building houses, and he said he'd sell me one. I told him I hadn't got the money. He offered to lend me the deposit if I could get a mortgage, so I went bravely down to the Halifax Building Society offices and faced the manager. He decided to trust me, too, so we started married life in a brand new house with £2.5s. a month to find for the mortgage and no job!'

A desperate situation, and Joe turned naturally for a solution to the land, the source of life for his kind for over a millennium. His grandfather had been a farmer and three of his brothers went to work on farms. He began to work his two allotments commercially and sought opportunities to get into the milk business.

'I thought to myself . . . well, lad, industry's done with you and you've done with it. I'll have a go at agriculture. I started to grow cabbages and if we had more than we could sell locally I'd sell 'em to the greengrocers. Eight pence a dozen, big-hearted cabbages. I got some poultry and a pig and then I swapped a portable gramophone for a goat, which meant I was in the milk business. It's surprising, but a good goat will give a gallon of milk. Word got around and people offered me more goats because everyone was on the make for a bob or two then — you had to, or else you couldn't live. All I could give to my wife for housekeeping when we first got married was eight shillings a week. Then we managed to acquire a cow. I put five pounds down and paid it off at a pound a month. The price was eighteen pounds, which is laughable today. But we had a big setback after we'd had her a year. I ordered some flake maize but I wasn't there when the chap delivered it and he just dumped it in the building where she was kept. The cow got loose and she bust herself on it. Died. So I was back where I started.'

The memory of that disaster still touches a nerve with Connie.

'We'd had to work so hard and save so hard,' she says, with feeling. 'It put us down on our knees. When one cow was all you had it was a serious matter.'

Joe's fighting spirit was not quenched, however, and he had another piece of luck when a businessman heard about the misfortune and asked if he knew where he could get another cow. Joe told him he could get one for fifteen pounds.

'Well, I can see you're trying, lad,' he said. 'I'll lend you the fifteen pounds at six per cent, to be paid back over a year.'

Joe was away again. However, he had a debt to pay, and just how hard that was can be judged from the fact that this immensely proud man still had not paid it off at the end of a year. He had to obtain a month's extension. But he would turn his hand to anything. When the weather was warm, he and Connie used laboriously to make ice-cream with the milk in a hand-cranked machine to sell on the streets of Guisborough and earn a few more coppers. The cow was kept in a henhouse on one of the allotments and Joe had to dig drains to satisfy the requirements of the local council, who sent their surveyor, the sanitary inspector and the medical officer to make sure that all by-laws had been complied with.

Hay for the cow was another major problem. Joe had no fields so he went out into the lanes with a scythe and cut the sides. When he built up his herd and began to breed heifers, getting enough hay became a tremendous burden.

'I got permission from the council to mow some of their land. And I went round offering to cut big lawns if I could keep the grass. I used to get several tons eventually, but it was a slow painful job.'

The sight of this grimly determined man carrying his scythe around the district searching for spare grass is still remembered. Sometimes, it is said, he was so tired at the end of the day that he scarcely had the strength to wrench his scythe free if the point jabbed into the ground.

He served a six-year apprenticeship to agriculture in this way and then in 1939 the established farming community accepted him. He was given the tenancy of Grange Farm, Girrick. Joe, Connie and their growing family marched eagerly down the narrow lane which slopes down to their farm accompanied by seven head of cattle, a few pigs and hens, less than one hundred pounds of capital but unlimited courage. Joe became the master of eighty acres of cold unfriendly land. The soil was not good. 'Never sow anything at Girrick before the second week in April,' was the advice offered.

Three decades later, the farm has fifty head of Jersey cows giving six churns of superb milk every day and his land is embellished with the spectacle of sixteen Cleveland Bay horses and gangling foals running thunderously free over his rolling acres in a way that would have excited the late Sir Alfred Munnings. Nothing else has changed. The buildings are probably much as they were a hundred years before Joe came, apart from an asbestos roofed shed. But that is how Joe likes it, for he is another who has no love for the tide of progress. There are few aids to modern living to ease the frugality of Grange Farm. Life generally is kept as it was in the past. Like other farmers, Joe was offered electricity but he turned it down. 'I like to keep things as simple as possible. Why make life any more complicated than it is! If we weren't milking by hand we'd only be doing something else. There's always a job looking at you on a farm. You could spend forty-eight hours every day and the work still wouldn't be done. Milking is quite a relaxing job, you know, and it gives you plenty of time to think. My mind goes round most problems, about everything in the world I should think.'

Connie, now in her sixties, clearly has a warmer opinion of electricity, but is hesitant to voice it strongly in deference to the master of the house.

'I had it all to leave when we came here. It took some doing, I can tell you. Electricity would be nice in a lot of ways, like for washing and things such as that. It's hard to know. I do all my washing by hand. But it's no good unless you're both of the same mind and we've managed all these years without it.

'Mind, it was worse than it is now, before we got the Calor gas. I had to heat the water for washing in the kitchen back boiler and I couldn't get it all done in one day then because I was washing for seven of us. We had five children in the house, you see.

'The hardest time we had came in the war because we had such a lot to do. We were obliged to grow corn and potatoes — oh, we were growing all the time there was and we got very tired. Then the children got up a bit and they started to help.

'But I was all right because I've had good health up to now. It doesn't bother me getting up at six o'clock and now most of the family's married I'd be lost if I didn't have outside work to do. Well, there's nothing else to do, really, because we can't get out much. There isn't the time.'

Obviously, Joe was a strict father to his children. They still all regard him with awe, even those who are married with homes and children of their own. Joe says he applied those stern principles of his by setting an example and having Bible readings when time permitted. He claims that he did not impose his views on them, he just told them 'what was right'. About corporal punishment he declares:

'You know what it says in the Good Book—spare the rod and spoil the child. If you beat them, they won't die. The rod of correction drives the foolishness from them. Apply those principles and you can't go far wrong.'

Joe says that he had no need to use the rod of correction very much on his children, but he certainly needs it from time to time with his Cleveland Bays, particularly when he is assembling them to go on display at the local annual shows. They have a wildness about them which cuts a wonderful dash down the fields because most of them are unbroken. Nobody rides them now, although Joe used to when he first took an interest in the breed. He was fortunate to get a start with Clevelands because the established breeders snap up any good horses that come on the market. But when he did acquire a good young stallion, Joe predictably fell in love with Clevelands and today stands alongside America Welford, Ruth Kitching and the other rulers of the Society. That first Cleveland cost him ten pounds from Sir Alfred Pease's stud, where his grandfather had worked as a horseman—yet another example of the lines of continuity which lace rural life together in Yorkshire.

The Cleveland Bay inspires Joe's prolific pen, which sometimes has Ruth Kitching struggling for space in the Society's magazines as she also tries to include the poetic fancies of America and herself. The creation Joe is most likely to declaim from (from memory) went into the very first issue of the magazine:

> The Cleveland Bay, an ancient breed
> Older than blood or thoroughbred
> Has served man's ever changing needs,
> His placid nature proven by deeds.
>
> With good blue feet and iron-hard limbs
> His sturdy courage never dims.
> With flexed knee and tireless tread
> He keeps on going when others drop dead.
>
> When roads were nought but moorland track
> He bore large loads upon his back
> To till the land they bred him short
> With sloping shoulders to ride for sport.
>
> Then with the roads the carriage came
> They bred him long for the harness game.
> But he still went on with tireless tread
> Earning mortal man his daily bread.

EAST OF THE CLEVELAND HILLS: Harbourside scenes at (top) Whitby about a century ago, and (below) in more recent times at Staithes, where Staithes bonnets are still worn. (Photos: The Sutcliffe Gallery and John Tindale)

MASTERS OF HORSE: America Jack Welford. Long training is needed for a horse to accept a sheep on its back.
Opposite: The village of Beckhole, near Goathland, between Whitby and Pickering. (Jack Wetherby)

George Nelson showing the three-year old Cleveland Bay colt 'Dalesman' to the Glaisdale Hounds. (John Tindale)

Ruth Kitching's Cleveland Bay stallion 'Chapman' in his summer coat. (Daphne Machin Goodall)

Left: Ruth Kitching, photographed about forty years ago.
Right: Hazel Nelson, aged ten, with a pair of two-year old Cleveland Bay colts. (John Tindale)

Left: Joe Sunley as a youth.

Right: A more recent photograph of Joe.

Below: Joe (left) with his four brothers.

Joe Sunley's 'Gerrick Thistledown', drawing the royal carriage as nearside wheeler (back, right) in 1965. (John Tindale)

Grange Farm, Girrick, home of Joe Sunley since 1939.

Joe Sunley carefully looks over one of his horses.

Another Yorkshire breed developed
With lighter frame and one that galloped.
The craze for speed had now begun,
So these two breeds were crossed to run.

Unheard of speeds were now attained
Their prowess noted became world-famed.
The world moved on: then came the cars.
The breed survived for men's leisure hours.

They were trained to jump which they enjoyed —
In other events they were employed.
So if you want a horse to ride,
To go all day and never bide,

To jump and jump and never falter,
To draw a carriage for Queen or Maltster,
A Cleveland Bay is what you're after,
The world's best horse with you as master.

Joe's passion for the Cleveland Bay happened to blossom at an important time for the breed. When the tractor drove the horse from the land in the 'forties and 'fifties he kept faith with his fast-growing and ever-improving stud. Even when the tractor was eventually allowed on his farm, all it meant was that his Clevelands had less work to do. There was no such sentiment on other farms and there came a time when only a handful of brood mares and proven stallions remained. Thus Joe can be numbered as another saviour of the breed.

In those days, Joe's constant companion was a stallion called Lucifer, who is remembered with great affection at Girrick.

'He was one of the good old sort, you know, I worked him from 1939 to 1947, yoking him three times a day, yet he'd still come home hard as nails with me on his back. And when the big snow came in 1947 and cut us all off I rode him through it to try and get some bread. Aye, it was a rough journey, that. Sixteen miles we travelled and we still couldn't find any bread. He was very tired when we got back home, but not as tired as me. I took him into the stable and started to go up the ladder to the loft to get him some hay when I began to tremble all over. My wife had to fodder him that night.'

Joe's skill at breeding fine Clevelands has earned him a personal meeting with the Queen at Windsor and international recognition. One of his best mares, which won the yearling filly class at the Great Yorkshire Show in 1956, went into the Royal Mews, and gave birth to two sons which help pull the royal coaches today. When the Queen came to York in 1971 for the city's 1900th anniversary celebrations she specially requested that her carriage be drawn by Cleveland

Bays, to honour the breed in its native land. Emperor Hirohito of Japan, another Cleveland enthusiast, bought a stallion from Joe to improve his bloodline and the Government of Pakistan have also been customers. The Japanese are particularly anxious to better their strain and are regular visitors to Grange Farm.

What passed between Her Majesty and this brooding man of the moors with the weather-lashed countenance remains a secret Joe will not divulge. But it must have been a remarkable moment of communication. She concluded the meeting by handing him a special rosette to commemorate the occasion, which was added to the bucketfuls Joe collects without pause at competitions ranging from the Royal Show to annual village affairs.

In 1973, the family of the late Wilkinson Keenleyside, who also played a major part in the promotion of the breed, gave a silver trophy to the Society, to be awarded to the breeder with the highest number of points won at recognised shows, excluding championships. It is known as the Showman of the Year Award and Joe became the first holder.

Down the years, Joe has bred over sixty Clevelands and he admits that his horses play an important part in the economy of the farm — 'the cows provide our bread and butter, the horses a bit of jam from time to time' — but he is reluctant to discuss prices, particularly that paid by the Queen.

'I got what I asked for,' is all he will say. But the Queen's Equerry wrote a complimentary letter, asking if Joe had any more as good.

There is no room for argument or coercion once Joe Sunley has made up his mind. For him, the issues of life are clearcut and he will suffer anything to defend his particular values. Challenge his views and his actions if you will, but he is a Compleat Man who commands the total respect of everyone who can recognise absolute honesty and inflexible character. With men like America Jack Welford, he protects with a fine ferocity the established virtues of Cleveland life, whether horse, land or people.

Sunley's Daughter

Joe Sunley's daughter Mary is a delicate, spindly roe-deer of a girl, as shy as any wild creature of the fields. The world outside her father's farm has touched her so little that casual communication is almost impossible. She has been nowhere, experienced little, has no friends.

She goes about life with a strained, preoccupied look, and well she might. Her father is now an old man with failing strength and despite her slight stature, Mary has to shoulder the main burden of work. But she does it willingly, for her loyalty to her parents transcends everything. She is extremely attractive. Indeed, on the occasions when her cares melt away for a fleeting moment, she smiles and displays a startling beauty.

Mary Sunley is a prisoner of circumstance. She is the last child of the Sunley's — all the others, including her twin brother, have left Grange Farm to lead their own lives. If Mary went, the pattern of work on the farm would collapse. Even Joe would admit this. Mary is honouring a Dales tradition, which has resisted change in East Cleveland more than in any other rural area, that one child must stay behind to care for the ageing parents. Usually it is the youngest daughter, or the last daughter to win a man. This has led to some tragic situations in years gone by, repeated at least once in recent memory, when a man died aged well into his fifties. The funeral was attended by the grief-stricken figure of a maiden lady, his fiancée for more than twenty years.

In these Dales, it was once usual for a man to start carving marriage spoons when his proposal was accepted by his lady love. He would select a very long piece of wood and begin by carving a wooden spoon. And then, without breaking the piece, he would fashion a link for every year of the engagement. When, or if, the match was finally made, he would finish the chain with another spoon to symbolise their undying union.

Above the roaring log fire in the Fox and Hounds at Ainthorpe, near Danby, there are a pair of marriage spoons carved about fifty years ago. The chain has twelve links. It is believed there are several more lying discarded and unfinished in attics and cellars, well seasoned memorials to romances that failed to withstand the strain of waiting. And it is said that an elderly swain in a Dale not far away

43

from the Fox and Hounds is rheumatically carving one today. If so, there will be nearly twenty links in the chain. This plaintive custom seems to be peculiar to the Eastern Dales, and one theory says the idea was imported from Scandinavia. If so, it must be the only contribution the sea was allowed to make to the life of these parts.

Mary leads such an enclosed and totally involved life that the chances of her ever meeting a young man in a situation where a romance could develop appeared very limited. But one day when she was twenty-two, a muscular young man with a monkish haircut and hands like shovels, strode down the lane to Girrick. Jim Smith had come to work at Low Farm, which adjoins the Sunley spread.

For fully a year, they ignored each other. Then one evening, Jim looked up and saw Mary silhouetted against a ridge, leading a Cleveland Bay and its foal. And one hand began to shake . . . and then the other. He could not stop them shaking.

A year later they became engaged. He wanted to get married almost straight away, but Mary said: 'No . . . wait'. In 1974, almost three years after that thunderbolt evening when Jim lost his heart, they were still waiting. She aged twenty-one, he thirty-one.

The story of their love affair and their agonising situation is the very stuff of poetry. Despite his years and apparent worldliness, Jim had never been out with a girl alone in his life until he courted Mary. As you would expect, he was the first suitor ever to enter Mary's life.

Jim was not consciously seeking an end to his celibate state that evening he watched Mary walk with the horses.

'I wondered what the devil was up with me at the time. My arm started jumping and twitching—it's a good job no one was around to see me. Then I couldn't sleep—I never slept for a week because I couldn't get her off my mind. A couple of days later when I was ploughing I noticed the hydraulics oil was getting low so I went to get a gallon can to fill it up.

'Instead of going back to the tractor I went to the pig sty and was about to pour it into the trough when I stopped myself. The poor pig was jumping up for an extra feed and I thought "What the hell am I doing here?" And when I did get back to the tractor it took me half an hour to find the place to put the oil in, although it was where it had always been. Thinking of Mary all the time I was. I reckoned it was time I was seeing the doctor, but I didn't dare because he would have laughed at me. Next day I started milking and I carried the first bucket away to the dairy, but went straight past and finished up in the pig house again with the sow jumping up for another extra feed. So I thought that day—it's no good, it's got the best of me. I must do something about it.

'That night I went straight up to their farm. I saw her mum and dad and asked for Mary and they told me she was milking. I went into the byre and found her hiding under a cow, but she stuck her head out and smiled at me before ducking away again. So I waited until they'd all finished milking — I hung about for a good hour or more. Then outside their back door I asked her to go out with me. She seemed hardly struck, and just said "Well, if you like . . . I don't mind . . . as long as I can get my milking done before we go out".

'That first night we went playing bowls in Middlesbrough and she was as quiet as a lamb. I was frightened to say a word wrong. It was like handling delicate china.'

But before long Mary was in love, too. The hugely happy Jim wanted to shout it aloud but she restrained him. They must wait 'at least a year' before the betrothal. This new shatteringly sudden turn of events had to be considered carefully in the light of her situation, and there had been nothing in her life to prepare her for dealing with it. It must have been her turn for sleepless nights.

Her father's farm had filled her life to the exclusion of all else since she could remember. At the amazingly early age of three she had begun to work in the cowshed, her infant fingers doing their best to squeeze the milk out of the udders. She was above five when her father had donned his stern new beliefs and there were no more birthdays or Christmases in the house to relieve the ceaseless toil.

When schooldays arrived, she had jobs to do before she started the long walk up the lane, and there were more on her return. Her affection was given to the animals for she did not find it easy to make friends, although she struck up a relationship with two girls she sat next to at school. But they never came to play on the farm, and when schooldays finished so did the friendship. However, she knows and loves all the animals on the farm, including the cows, and can reel off their names instantly — Sapphire, Starlight, Willow, Candy, Cindy, Goldie and so on — and remembers with clear affection a Shetland pony called Wendy which her father bought for his children when they were young. She does not like to talk about the day it had to be sold to a riding school because they had all grown too big for it. No more does she like to talk about the time when a cow becomes too old to be of any further use and the knacker comes to take it away.

She admits she had no real friends outside the family until Jim appeared all hot and bothered in the cow byre that evening, and she declares that she has not missed them.

'You never miss what you've never had,' she says, without a trace of self pity.

Most of the influences that shape other people have passed her by. She had no records to play or television to dominate her, so the Beatles, John F. Kennedy, the Moon walkers and the three-day week came and went without causing so much as a ripple in her life.

'I don't know anything else but farming, do I? I've no hobbies because I work on the farm full-time and I haven't left it much. I went to stay with an aunt in Leeds once when I was about nine — I found it a very busy place — but that's about all. Oh yes, I did go to Scotland on a day trip once. We all went in the car because my brother wanted to see something but I can't remember where we went. We got up early and did the milking before we set off and again when we got back. That's the only time I've been out of England. I've never been to London and I haven't much desire to go.'

Although she and Jim live and work within fifty yards of each other they do not have as much contact as other couples.

'We go out together about three times a week. But I can't meet Jim until the work's done after nine o'clock so we're not able to go to the pictures or anything like that. I haven't been to the pictures much, but I've watched television at his parents' place. Sometimes we go to a pub but I only drink lime and lemon, and sometimes we go to a dance at one of the village halls.'

Mary does not talk easily and turns to ice if any criticism of her father is implied. She refuses to discuss the relationship. It is equally painful for her to discuss her plans for her future with Jim.

'We'll get married when it's convenient, as soon as the situation changes and makes it possible. I can't just leave, can I?'

It was exactly a year after she and Jim first went out together that Mary agreed to become formally engaged. They went down one Saturday morning to Middlesbrough to pick the ring.

'It was a lovely year, that day,' recalls Jim, quaintly. 'Mary took so long choosing a ring — three hours I think it was — and when we got back the cows were coming down the lane for milking.

'She took the ring home and never said anything. Anyway, after tea and when all the work had been finished I went up there. Mary came straight to me, and then got the ring out — it was still wrapped up in its little box — and showed it to her mum and dad. They didn't say much. I think they were stuck for words. In fact, I don't think her dad said anything at all, but her mum wished us all the best of luck.

'Then we went off to see my parents. Mother was bad in bed at the time, but she was over the moon about it and gave Mary a kiss. It almost made her better there and then. I know that the reception we got at Mary's farm was a lot different but it was more or less expected. It didn't worry me, though, because it was a choice of ours, not theirs. It wouldn't have made any difference had they objected to the engagement — it's a thing they will have to like or lump.'

Jim is very much his own man but is understandably wary of Joe Sunley. He believes that Joe should get a milking machine — 'it's just hard work and it takes up so much time which could be spent doing other jobs. Anyway, if he got one Mary and me could get out earlier on a night.

'But we get on all right. We don't argue because I've found out that it just isn't worthwhile arguing with folks with strong opinions.'

It is a very cautious relationship on both sides. Ask Joe what he thinks of Jim and he replies: 'Why should I pass any remarks about him? He's all right as far as I know. He took to Mary, she took to him. He's her choice. I don't really know the lad. You know, in the old days parents used to pick the marriage partners for their children and I think it was quite a good system. Well, when you've been around a bit you've seen a bit, haven't you? Very often young people rush into marriage and it's not long before they're getting divorced.'

Connie Sunley thinks Jim is a 'very fair, decent man, as much as I've seen of him. . . . I don't think he smokes and doesn't drink a lot to my knowledge. They should be happy.' Even Joe, who says that the ideal sort of man for a daughter of his to marry would be 'someone who abides by Bible principles', indicates a general approval of the match. Any reluctance on their part is clearly due in the main to worries about the vast problems Mary will leave in her wake when she leaves for the altar. Most farmers as old as Joe would settle for semi-retirement, but his wife says with a patience born of a lifetime by his side: 'He won't give in, you know.'

It is doubtful whether Joe has worked out a solution. 'We would have to adjust,' he says, slowly. 'The two of us couldn't milk all those cows. I don't really know what we'll do until we come to it.' He is sure that Mary will come back and help with the work, if at all possible, even when she does get married, although Mary admits any such arrangements would not be popular with Jim. Both Connie and Joe insist that they are not holding Mary back, and Joe repeats the phrase which his father uttered when he went to talk to him about his own long-shelved plans to marry Connie: 'Everyone has their own life to live.'

The decision rests with Mary, and it obviously casts a shadow on her life. It hangs there permanently, except for the three or four times a week when work is behind her and her slight figure is swept into Jim's huge embrace. And they can dream their dreams of a farm of their own and the two children they want, and wander the lanes and fields in rosy oblivion.

To see them come together like this is both a privilege and an emotional strain, for they radiate a desperate joy which would tear the heart of Montagu or Capulet.

Jim's longing for the only girl ever to touch his life has driven him to suggest a move to Scotland or even abroad—anywhere where they can be together. But Mary has sadly turned down every plan. They could consummate their romance in a rent-free, rate-free, completely modernised cottage on one of the big farms a few miles away from Grange Farm, for Jim's agricultural skill is known in the area. But even that is too far for Mary at the moment.

'I know we're only forty yards apart,' says Jim with a rare anguish. 'But that's too far at times. I want to see Mary in the morning. And at night. And during the day too. I want to see her all the time. But I can't tell you when we will marry. It's like counting plumstones

—this year . . . next year . . . sometime . . . never.'

Next to becoming man and wife, Mary and Jim yearn most of all for a small farm of their own. But the prospect of their ever having this dream fulfilled hardly exists.

For the land is being taken from the people.

It never belonged to them in title, drenched though it is in a thousand years of their sweat, joy and misery. The great landlords, whose ancestors often took it by the sword or secured it by indulging the whims of a monarch, never completely released their grip. But for many centuries they have ruled their domains with a benevolent despotism, which at least gave a man a fair chance to rear his crops and cattle with security of tenure and peace of mind. When a family put its roots down in a piece of land, they were generally allowed to stay, generation after generation. The eldest son traditionally took over from his father, and even the more ambitious younger brothers usually managed to find a vacant tenancy. And businesslike men, who worked and saved and knew how to secure a mortgage, could always find a freehold farm within their financial reach.

During the last decade, a disturbing and determined start has been made to dismantle this comfortable old structure. To be fair, it must be said that the squirearchy is being forced by all kinds of pressures in this, and it's likely that it is done with reluctance.

The *malaise* seized the free and independent farms first of all. They command outrageous prices. For a modest spread which would have cost less than five thousand pounds fifteen years ago, Jim would have to find at least thirty to forty thousand pounds. An entire generation of young men, yeomen all, are in danger of being driven away from the Dales. The implications scarcely bear thinking about.

To stay on the land, Jim's sole alternative is to persuade the agent of one of the aristocracy who own the enormous, multi-farm estates which proliferate in the Yorkshire Dales to grant him a tenancy. He tried this, in an interview with the agent who acts for the owners of a breathtaking slice of East Cleveland which includes all the farms in Girrick, including Joe Sunley's.

This particular agent is a wise and able administrator who is well aware of Jim's sturdy character and wide experience. He was most sympathetic. But he could offer nothing — not even the faint prospect of a farm to let. He explained that the price of houses and the rising cost of living is putting the luxury of retirement beyond the pocket of many small farmers. And when the landlord does get occupation it is usually the first chance he has had in thirty years to adjust the size of neighbouring farms or bring in new blood.

He went on to expound a theory about farm size which is held by many large landowners and their agents:

'The question of farm size is vitally important, particularly now we are in the Common Market. We have to ensure our farms are viable, and it would be no use putting you on a farm which could bankrupt you within ten years.

'A viable unit will vary in size, according to the quality of the land. For instance, up at Cirrick I would like to see four to five hundred acres as one farm.'

The interview concluded with the agent wishing Jim success in trying to raise enough capital to buy his own farm.

Without blaming this particular agent and his landlord, who are now forced to think in terms of Europe and not just half a Dale, Jim is understandably bitter about the situation.

'The government's encouraging them to amalgamate, you know. The landlords get a cash grant and outgoing tenants are often given a golden handshake. It isn't a bit fair, really. No-one's bothered about the small farmer now. It's all big business with farms being turned into companies, and I think it's bad for the country to put all this land into the hands of a few people.'

Landlords have other opportunites to exploit amalgamations. When an adjoining farm is handed over to a favoured tenant, he takes the land and the farm buildings but has no need of the farm-house. So it can be sold for a large sum to a stockbroker or rich lawyer as a country home — local people can rarely afford to buy such desirable rural retreats.

The implications of the agent's explanation to Jim are serious for Joe Sunley, too. Clearly, the landlord would like to weld together two or three farms at Girrick, which means that Grange Farm is hardly likely to remain within Joe's gift. He probably will not be able to arrange for Mary and Jim to follow him, or be able to nominate one of his other children (more than one of whom would dearly like a farm).

A handful of tenants managed to foresee the trend and skilfully arranged for a son's name to go on the rent book by taking him into partnership, thus preserving security of tenure for another generation. Many more thought of doing the same but could not bring themselves to choose between their children, even if they were old enough to make it practical. Now the opportunity has, by and large, vanished.

With his physique and intelligence, Jim knows he could secure a high-wage job at the potash mines around Whitby, which have partially filled the alternative employment gap left by the demise of the iron-ore mines, but he also realises that he would be miserable underground after a free life in the open air. He was born and brought up on a farm and is not the sort of man you could imprison in industry.

And as Mary says, 'It's no good changing your job if farming's what you want to do and makes you happy. Money doesn't mean

49

everything.'

So she and Jim prepare to go forward into life stripped of the birthright granted to their parents, with a pair of blankets in their bottom drawer and not much else materially. They seem destined to join the lost legion of young countrymen and women now forlornly trying to find a tenancy in the Dales.

Unless there is legislation to help them they will be forced to abandon their heritage and leave the valleys to the corporation men. The potential damage to a social structure which has survived wars, famines and the industrial revolution is incalculable, conjuring up a nightmare vision of a beautiful but dead prairie land echoing to the voices not of people but of monstrous agricultural machines.

Muscle, Soothing Whistles and Curious Oaths

Forty years ago in the summer streets of Guisborough, one of the children who carried pennies for Joe Sunley as he sold ice-cream wearily made by hand from the milk yielded by his one cow, was a slim lad called Scott Blowman, son of a foundry worker.

Young Scott sported an ambition to be an electrical engineer at the time, but when his headmaster secured an interview for him at the age of fourteen the gods who care for the ancient roots of this land intervened. On the appointed evening, he boxed at the Boys' Club and did not bother to go home and change into his Sunday clothes. The year was 1939 when these things mattered, so he did not get the job.

He is using his muscle to this day as he bestrides a vital rural industry like a colossus, the last of his kind in Guisborough, medieval capital of Cleveland. Scott Blowman, blacksmith, is a comforting sight to those who believe that such men should fulfil the image bestowed upon them by song and fable.

Scott projects a chest which measures forty-eight inches in repose, and an anvil hammer in his hand looks like the delicate instrument sweet shop owners once used to shatter treacle toffee. It is a truly awesome sight to see him shoe an unruly Cleveland Bay. The meeting becomes a veritable clash of giants as he wrestles the animal, his biceps matching the horse's thigh inch for inch, and utters a mixture of soothing whistles and curious oaths. Into the clang and clamour of his forge at Newstead Farm, where the sparks spray like windblown rain from the tortured fluorescent steel fresh from the fire, come a constant stream of people urgently requiring his craft. Butchers with ruptured sausage machines, shipbuilders who want boilers welded, children with broken toys, and horses of all kinds. He treats them all impartially and with boisterous good humour.

Although Scott has mastered all the new technology in smithying, he believes in the traditional methods and still forges his own horseshoes from steel bars instead of buying them ready pressed. He was trained in a hard school at the hand of one of the Dale family who were once the rulers among the regiment of blacksmiths who competed for business in East Cleveland at the turn of the century. Pride in the job was ferocious in those days and the Dales, all six of them, were renowned for their skill and spread their forges all around Guisborough. Herbert Dale, the father of the clan, revelled in their supremacy.

'I never knew him,' says Scott, 'but he is still talked about. He would please himself whether he took your job or not and if he didn't like the look of you then you'd be sent packing. But he used to take a savage delight in shoeing a horse nobody else could tackle, just to show them all.'

The power of the Dales was broken during the First World War when four of the sons were killed and another died later from his wounds. Their father did not survive these blows and died himself shortly afterwards. But it was to Herbert Dale, junior, that Scott applied for a job when his plans to become an electrical engineer went sour.

'I asked him if I was to sign indentures and serve my time, but he told me that I would get a month's trial and I wouldn't even last that long if I wasn't good enough. He was a hard master—he'd show you how to do a job once, and that was it. I remember when I was sixteen I decided to cut and weld a steel tyre for a wooden wheel on my own. I wasn't supposed to at that age but Mr Dale was out, you see. I didn't do it right because it came out shaped like an egg instead of being perfectly round. He was the only one in the shop who had the ability to straighten it out but when he came back and saw it he said: "Whoever did that can put it right" and walked out again. I was nearly in tears and none of the other apprentices dared help me but I set to and sweated over that thing, which weighed a hundredweight, for three hours. But by the time he came back I'd even got it on the wheel. It was a good way to learn and I was allowed to do more after that.

'Hooping wheels was a hell of a job because they were all fire-welded out of four-and-a-half-inch wide steel, an inch thick. We had to throw them straight on the wooden wheel glowing red from the fire and then splash cold water on to stop the wood from burning and shrink the metal to leave the wood proud. If you weren't quick enough ash would form between the wood and metal and you'd lose all the nip.'

Before the honour of hooping at such an early age was conferred upon him, Scott had another near disaster with wheels. The wheel-wright's shop was just down the road in the centre of Guisborough and his apprentices used to bring the wheels across to the blacksmith's on a handcart. When the hoops were seared on, the finished wheels were bowled down the road back to the wheelwright's.

'First time I had to deliver one I tried to be smart and start to bowl the wheel down the road from the side instead of from behind. Now this wheel stood nearly five foot high and weighed around two and a half hundredweight, and I forgot there was a nice slope down to the wheelwright's. Well, I lost control and it started bowling down to the junction with the main road—just as a single-decker bus was approaching. It would have just nicely hit it—and it could have taken the side clean off—but I slapped the wheel with the flat of my hand . . . and shut my eyes. When I opened them again I saw the wheel was following the contour of the road and running alongside the bus. I raced across the pavement to cut it off and there was no damage, but by heck it frightened me.'

When Scott was a youth, the centre of Guisborough was a warm, bustling place given over to crafts now virtually extinct. There were five forges all competing for business, but there was plenty of work for all because the horse was still the king of the road.

'I saw the tail end of that era,' says Scott. 'Everyone had horses. The Co-op, for instance, had four cart-horses pulling their coal carts and used ponies for their milk floats and vans. They did have an old Thornycroft wagon but it was only used one day a week and all the rest of the work was done by horses. There was one marvellous old character on the Co-op coal wagons called "Coaly" Wilkinson who used to go belting down the streets with his horse shouting "Coal today . . . coal today!" The pride of the Co-op in those days was a big Clydesdale gelding called Captain, the most outstanding horse on the streets of Guisborough. He was all beautifully done out with brass gear and everybody looked at him when he went out and about. Now my boss, Herbert Dale, always shod this horse personally, and it had to be done as an advert for our forge. All the other smiths used to keep their eyes on it and if they'd spotted anything—say, one shoe was a sixteenth of an inch out in the one eighth of an inch coverage round the hoof—there would have been hell on.

'When I started striking for Mr Dale I was allowed to pull Captain's shoes off and dress his feet but I never nailed on. And he was shod every six weeks, religiously. Well, one day Mr Dale went to a funeral and Captain came in unexpectedly for shoeing. So I took his old ones off and dressed him. When I asked when Mr Dale would be back I was told me might not be returning that day. The other two shoeing smiths at our place refused to touch him so we hung on until four o'clock, hoping he would come back. Then I said that I would have to do it because Captain was due on his rounds the following day. I was just clinching the last foot off when one of the other smiths ran in saying that the old man was coming up the street. "He'll go crackers when he sees what you've done," he said. Well, he walked in and stopped dead when he saw Captain newly shod. Then he looked at me and said: "Are you satisfied with that, then?" I said I thought I could have improved one of the back feet. We discussed it for a bit and then he said "Humph! You haven't made a bad job of it," which was a big compliment from him.

'Anyway, from that day on he never shod Captain any more. I did it. I really took pride in the job and used to file the edge of the shoes until they looked as though they were chrome-plated. But I didn't get any more compliments from the old man. In fact, six months later someone was admiring the way Captain was shod and telling Mr Dale what a good job I was doing but all he said was "Well, look who showed him how to do it!"'

The time was fast approaching when the tractor drove the horse from the land and the fires in the forges were gradually snuffed out. Scott recalls that evolution with regret.

'Nearly all the horses went. Most of them for beef. Even Captain was shot.'

However, proud Captain and his companions enjoyed their lives, curtailed though they were. There were other horses around Guisborough which very clearly did not. They led harsh and miserable lives a thousand feet underground in the ninety-seven iron ore mines which heaped their sores around a fifteen-mile radius of the town. Eight of them were dotted over the moors along the road between Scott's forge and Joe Sunley's farm at Girrick, a route Scott has followed for twenty years to shoe Joe's Cleveland Bays.

'They didn't have pit ponies because there were no thin seams like you have in coal mines. You could get cart horses down there and each mine had around sixteen Clydesdales, which could haul ten or twelve tubs at one time. It wasn't good work for them because their legs would go what we call "greasy", covered in a green slime which used to hang down like bunches of grapes. It was caused by all the damp and sulphur and they used to suffer most during cold winters when the frost got into the cracks in their legs. They also got canker in the foot for which there was no cure. It was always a terrible job shoeing 'em because of the smell from the slime. You had to wrap their legs with sacks because if any of it got on your clothes they had to be burned. These horses had to be shod very tight because if you left a lip on the shoe there was always something to catch on down a mine, like the sleepers between the rail lines.

'Their hooves were even more troublesome. The canker would eat out the complete inside of their foot and we'd have to put a steel plate across and seal it with Stockholm tar to stop stones getting inside. Mind you, they wouldn't feel much there and they were always carefully looked after by the vet. But you couldn't stop accidents, of course, and some of them would get crushed or have their legs smashed by a breaking pit prop and they would have to be shot.

'They never saw daylight, except when the pit stopped for the annual holidays. They were stabled down there, and even had their own smithy. When they were brought up their eyes had to be protected against the light for a bit, but it was marvellous to see them when they felt the grass under their feet again. They used to gallop around and act like babies, big as they were.'

By the early 'fifties all the ironstone mines had closed down and most of the surviving horses were sold for beef. But a few went on

54

to live a normal lifespan on the farms, and one became perhaps the best known horse in Guisborough. Billy, a small Clydesdale gelding, was bought by a greengrocer and carried fruit and vegetables to his customers until his groom died more than fifteen years ago. He was retired to pasture and loved his freedom so much that he refused to come back in again, allowing few people except children to approach him. Successive generations of Guisborough children had their first horse ride on the woolly back of amiable old Billy. In early 1974 he was still roaming his field happily at the age of about thirty-six.

By the time he was a young man, Scott had become an acknowledged master of his craft, able to do any job that came into the smithy. Herbert Dale came to rely on him more and more and had agreed to hand the business over to him eventually.

'But he was a hard and stubborn man. Small, about five feet five but very strong, he was brilliant with horses because he started life as a groom. He was a real dandy and loved dressing up in the latest fashion, but he never married. He lived with his sister, who also never wed, so a great line of blacksmiths died out with them. He wouldn't let go of the business even when he was retired. I was a young man and very hard up because all I got was about twenty-five shillings a week, so I'm afraid we had a big row. He wouldn't sell me the business and I just couldn't wait any longer.'

Then a remarkable thing happened to Scott. Along the same street there was another blacksmith called Albert Woodhouse, who worked in stern rivalry with his neighbours — and in those days combatants in business cut each other dead. But Scott, always a generous soul, maintained friendly relations with all the other local blacksmiths. Mr Woodhouse retired, and when he heard about Scott's problem he came to him and said: 'I know we've been business rivals, but you're the only man who has been a friend of mine since I came here. Take my shop.'

The astonished young blacksmith found himself the proprietor of a forge in less time than it took to cross the street. 'He just gave it to me,' says Scott, still breathless about the incident after twenty-five years. 'Not sold it to me — gave! Tools, anvils, the lot. I'm still using his anvil today.'

Scott was able to get married on the strength of his new-found independence but in a short time he ran into more trouble. The shop was only a small one and he desperately needed to expand, but could not get permission. Then he was told that the place had to be demolished.

'Well, the wife and I decided to emigrate. Word got around about this and it reached the Brunton family, marvellous people who farmed in a big way. The late Mr Norman Brunton came to me and asked why I was leaving, so I told him I had no premises. "Well, we can't do without a blacksmith, Scotty," he said. 'I'll build vou a smithy." So he did, alongside his farm and formed a company. But they just let me get on with it—I hardly ever see the Bruntons. There couldn't be better people to work with.'

So Scott Blowman has been rescued twice by the people of Guisborough and he swears he will never desert them now, although he has been offered one job worth £150 a week with foreign travel thrown in. He is an ornamental smith of wide renown who has exhibited in London and whose work adorns several churches.

'But I have a duty to stay here. The blacksmith's and the cobbler's have always been places to congregate on wet days in the country and folk still gather in my place now. Children bring their problems to me, and their broken toys. People expect me to do anything, and they have a right. I've mended false teeth, put back eyes into dolls, welded broken spectacles together, everything. I may get four thousand-pound jobs doing work on ships' boilers but I'm still the village handyman.

'You know, the other day a grand little lad at the top of the village broke his bike. In two pieces, it was. Do you know, he walked all the way here down by the beckside carrying those two pieces, looked at me and said: "You'll mend it, won't you?"

'Of course, I did—for a thank you. It's things like that which make me realise how much I'm needed here.'

SUNLEY'S DAUGHTER: Mary Sunley at the Great Yorkshire Show in 1959 with the gelding 'Emeralda'.

Mary and her twin brother Edmund as babies.

Above: Mary Sunley at work on Grange Farm.
Opposite, top: Father and daughter.
Opposite, bottom: The Sunleys with some of Joe's innumerable awards.

Mary Sunley and Jim Smith.

Mary with her dog Sadie in the bottom meadows.

Wedding-day picture of Jim Smith
and Mary Sunley.

The Smiths' daughter Diane, aged
nine months.

AUNT CISSIE:
Cissie's husband William Thompson, aged 81.

THE WORLD'S BIG__ GEST GOOSEBERRY:
George Harland (seated) the year he won the cup at the Egton Bridge Old Gooseberry Show.

A VERY SPECIAL DALESMAN: George Harland, self-taught historian, naturalist and archaeologist, seen (above) as a young stonemason (the left-hand figure in the picture), and (below) on the double bass with the Glaisdale String Orchestra.

THE BALLAD OF BEGGAR'S BRIDGE: A tragedy at the bridge, when a horse hung itself after inexplicably leaping over the side.

Skating at the bridge in the hard winter of 1893, when it snowed almost continuously for 13 weeks from Christmas Eve onwards.

Aunt Cissie

On 31 March 1875, Disraeli was in Number Ten and annoying Queen Victoria, America was just recovering from the effects of the Civil War and Cecily Hilda Thompson was born at Number 102 Westgate, Guisborough.

On 31 March 1974, Cecily Hilda nonchalantly entered her hundredth year with the energy of a woman half her age. A bright-eyed sparrow of a woman known everywhere as Aunt Cissie, she lives alone in her council bungalow a few yards away from her birthplace and darts around the streets of Guisborough, shopping and calling on friends and relatives. She is a great-aunt by marriage to Scott Blowman, and a blood relative of the Raws of Lawnsgate Farm in Eskdale.

To say that she looks after herself and her home is something of an understatement. She does so in a way which would exhaust most women half a century younger—just thinking about it. She still mangles her washing dry with an arm-powered antique and presses with an old flat iron, which has to be heated on a naked flame.

Most of her life was lived in the heart of Eskdale, first as a farmer's daughter and then as a farmer's wife. It was a time of hiring fairs, when men and women were treated only a little better than serfs, of unending poverty and of dawn to dusk work, using primitive implements. Transpose the Wessex setting to Yorkshire, and Aunt Cissie could have stepped from the pages of *Far From the Madding Crowd*.

Her memory is amazingly clear and precise.

'There were fourteen of us children, seven boys and seven girls, and I was one of the younger ones. The house in Guisborough only had two bedrooms. We had a very plain upbringing but we were always kept clean and I never recall going hungry. My father was Frank Raw Readman—his mother was a Raw from Fryup Dale—and he worked as a wood turner at the woodyard in Guisborough. I went to the Providence School where we had to pay twopence a week. We always had to have our twopence a week for school, even in the very hard times.

'My father fell out of work when I was nine. He walked miles trying to find another job but it was no use. But he always kept a cow in the field at the back of the house so we had plenty of milk, and some to sell. And my mother took in lodgers to help out a bit. After a while Father gave up hoping for another job and took a small-holding at Lealholm. I can still remember the removal day. A wagon drawn by two horses came for the furniture and we stopped off on the way at my Aunt Bessie's at Little Moorsholm to bait the horses. It was thirteen miles to our new place.

'There was thirty acres of land to go with it and life changed from then on. I still went to school at Lealholm for a bit but there was no more playing for us children. No time for games. We had to go out and work in the fields, doing all sorts. One of our jobs was to collect peat from the moor. We never burnt anything else on the fire. Father would cut it out and borrow Uncle George Readman's cart from Lealholm Hall, where he was farming in quite a big way. We children would load the cart and bring it down to the farmyard and stack the turves for winter. The cooking was done on the fire. We used to be very fond of melcake, which was made with currants and done in a pan with turves heaped on top of the lid.

'Father had three cows, some pigs and poultry and one horse, a grey mare called Polly. He was quite proud of Polly. We made butter and curds for market and he used to collect from the other farms round about and take the lot on the mare to Guisborough to sell at the market once a week. Eggs were twenty a shilling and butter eightpence a pound.

'We nearly lost the mare once when Lord Downe was out shooting on the moor nearby. He let a gun off near to Polly when she was pulling a sledge and she bolted, running straight for an old pitshaft. I thought she was sure to fall down it, but she pulled up just short. But one of her legs was all torn open when a chain wrapped round it and Father had to call the farrier to come.

'The work was very hard. We had to pick wittens (grass roots) out of the fields and make piles of them for burning. Hay and corn we cut with a scythe. The threshing we did with a flail, which I used many a time. You had to mind how you swung one of them or you would clout yourself on the head with it. Then we would rake up the corn and put it into a wooden winnowing machine to separate it. It was turned by hand.

'When he was about ten, George, my younger brother, was helping my father with the winnowing machine one night, working by lantern light. I was in the house with my mother when George suddenly came in groaning and holding his hand. He had caught a finger in the cog wheels and it was just hanging on with a bit of skin. Father was going down next day to Guisborough with the butter and eggs so he took him to the doctor, who cut it off. George always had a bit of bone sticking out of that finger from then on. But the poor lad went and died at fourteen from consumption of the bowels, and after that I had to take on his work as well.'

The farm was more isolated than most and Cissie had to walk a mile to the nearest shop if the family required anything. It was also vulnerable to bad weather and one year they were cut off for six weeks.

'The snow was so deep that you could walk all the way to Lealholm on top of it and never see a wall, hedge, gate or stile or anything. Sometimes we would be badly hit at harvest by wet weather. The fields would flood over and we'd see the sheaves of corn swirling round in the water and being washed away. Them was catchy times, and there wouldn't be much money to come.'

The family rarely left the Dale and Cissie had to wait until she was eleven for her first view of the sea, close though it was. Her elder brother came home on holiday and decided to take Cissie and her younger brother down to Whitby for a treat.

'Of course, we were quite excited. I remember wondering whether the sea was bigger than the river or not. We couldn't understand when we finally got there why we couldn't see across to the other side'.

Naturally, communications were poor. Wars, elections and other happenings in the outside world came and went without evoking a great deal of interest in Eskdale.

'We were up on the moor, you see. Sometimes men came to visit my father and they would talk about matters other than farming. We heard about the Boer War and we used to get the *Whitby Gazette* once a week from the shop. But we hadn't much spare time. At nights I used to do quilting, make rugs and knit and sew. There was a woman at a farm nearby who had three or four sons at farm place and she would pay a shilling a time for shirts and socks to give her boys when they came home at Martinmas. They'd have a week off, you see, and then go back as servant boys to bigger farms.

'There was always a hiring fair at Egton on Martinmas Day (23 November). I remember going to one around 1890 when I was about sixteen. My Aunt Jane Anne at Lealholm Hall, whose family was better off than us, asked me to go with her one day, to hire a servant girl.

'Well, when we got there scores of young men and women were waiting to be hired. It was what everybody did in those days. As soon as their children left school they were buckled off to farm place. The farmers walked up and down the street examining the young men, asking them questions about what they could do. They thought I was looking for a place, too, and first one and then the other came up and asked me if I was to hire. I heard one farmer talking to a young man, saying he couldn't decide whether to take him. He would have to get his character first. When he came back he said: "Well, I've got your character now—" but before he had a chance to say anything else the lad says "Yes, and I've got yours, too!" and that was the finish of that.

'My aunt went up and down the girls and finally got suited. She gave her the hiring penny, which was usually two shillings or half a crown, and if you accepted that you were hired for the year until next Martinmas. The wages were generally five pounds a year and you worked seven days a week, getting up at four or five o'clock in the morning when times were busy, and going on until dark.'

The day soon came when Cissie had to go out to farm place herself. At the age of seventeen she was sent to a milk farm a few miles away at Grosmont, in an arrangement made previously by her parents.

'I'm afraid I got with a slave driver. She nearly worked me to death. I had to go out with the milk to the houses, leading a donkey with a can on either side of its back, and do just about everything else. Anyway, after three months of that I fell ill and my legs swelled up. The farmer's wife said I would be no good if I was going to be ill and she sent me home. I was glad to go, I'll tell you. My mother had to call in the doctor and when he saw me he demanded to know where I'd been sent to work. When he was told he said: "You want a good horsewhipping for sending her to a place like that."

'Then I went to become a servant girl for a retired parson at Aislaby and I nearly hungered to death there. He had a housekeeper and I think she was putting a bit into her own pocket. I wasn't treated badly but I didn't get enough to eat. Just porridge, tea and bread and butter. Hardly ever meat. One day the housekeeper was making scones, which she only did when company was coming, and they looked so good. I said "Oh — can't I have one?" but she replied: "I don't make scones for the likes of you!" I told her that at home we used to have currant cakes at breakfast. She said that my mother must have been a very extravagant woman, which made me mad because my mother never had anything to be extravagant with.

'I stayed there about six months, getting paid about half a crown a week, and then I had to go back home again because my young brother fell ill and I was needed to work on the farm. I had to be farm lad as well as farm lass because the others had either married or left home to work.'

Cissie used to wait on at her aunt's farm at Lealholm Hall when she was having guests, and among the regular visitors were the photographer Frank Meadow Sutcliffe and his wife. Sometimes he spent holidays at Lealholm Hall.

'I remember him well. He was a fine gentleman, very tall, with a beard, and he always wore a soft hat. He had a big camera with legs and he used to take pictures all over the place. Very interested in harvests and haytiming, he was. He took a very good one of my Uncle George using an old corn cutter. I also recall him taking one which you see all over the place now — that one called "Rake's Progress". He got this farm lad to put his arm round a servant girl who had a hay rake over her shoulder, just like they were courting. I knew those two, and they weren't.

'But he never took any pictures of me.'

Life for the teenage daughter of a small Eskdale farmer was not much fun as the last decade of the nineteenth century dawned. But two or three times a year Cissie was allowed to go out to a dance in the valley.

'I'll never forget my first dance. It was held after the Club walk, which was the biggest event of the year in the Dale. The Shepherds and the Oddfellows, two local societies, used to join together and march up to the head of the Dale behind a band and then go to a chapel for a service. On the way back as they marched to Lealholm we children would run in to various farms and houses to collect joints of meat and jugs of gravy to take to the Shepherds' Hall so that dinner would be ready when they arrived. It was a lovely time. There would be a dance at night and one year I was allowed to go. Everyone was very shy, the lads sitting at one side of the floor and the lasses at the other. Anyway, my brother, Thomas—the same one who took us to see the sea—came over and asked me to dance. He was a very good dancer. I wouldn't get up at first but he made me and I had my very first dance. I think it was a polka or a schottische. After that, one of the other young men came to ask me, and then another and another. I went to every dance I could after that.'

The kindly elder brother who regularly tried to broaden the horizons of his young sister was the pride of the family, for he went on to become a schoolteacher. But he, too, tragically died of consumption at the age of twenty-seven.

It was five years after that first heady dance before serious romance came to Cissie's life. She was twenty-two and there was another meal and dance down at the Shepherds' Hall to celebrate the Jubilee of Queen Victoria in 1897. She captivated a quiet man nine years her senior called William Thompson, who was cowman to Lord Normanby at Mulgrave Castle, Lythe.

'We went up to Danby Beacon together after the dance to see the bonfire. And that was the start of it. We were married within the year.'

Cissie's father was not at all pleased. He refused point blank to go to the wedding, for she was the last child to marry and this meant that his major help on the farm was being taken away. Another elder brother, John William, sprang to her side and gave her hand in marriage. There was no church in Lealholm at the time, so the party had to travel to Glaisdale.

'I went to my wedding on foot and by train. I had a nice new dress and a white hat and veil and we walked a mile to Lealham station to catch a train to Glaisdale. Then we walked another mile to the church where I married William in the afternoon. Afterwards, we all went back to my father's farm the same way and had tea.

My father had his tea with us, but didn't say anything.

'Next day I moved into William's cottage on the Mulgrave estate at Lythe. There was one room upstairs but we slept downstairs in a bed which folded away into a cupboard. There was no water in the house and we had to carry buckets from a tap down the village. The rent was half a crown a week and my husband's pay was eighteen shillings. He looked after the pigs and poultry for Lord Normanby as well as the cows and he had to make sure there were plenty of eggs and chickens for the Castle table all through the year. He was the deerman, too, and he used to kill a deer and carry it on his back to the Castle whenever his Lordship wanted venison.

'I enjoyed being at Lythe. It was a nice village. The Normanbys were good people and all the tenants and workers would be invited up to the Castle now and again for pantomimes and Christmas parties. I remember the young Lord getting married. When he came back off honeymoon he was met at Sandsend station by the men of the estate. They took the horses out of the carriage waiting for him and his bride, and pulled it all the way up Lythe bank to the Castle.

'Whenever something special happened for the Normanbys such as the birth of the child there was always the firing of the stiddy. The blacksmith fired it. He turned his anvil upside down and packed the little hollow in the base with gunpowder. He'd set it off two or three times at weddings and the birth of a son.

'We only stayed three years at Lythe. William wanted a bit more money; they couldn't give it to him so he took a smallholding alongside my father's place. At first, he had to get a job as a woodman for Sir Francis Lea, who was the big man round Lealholm way. Then we managed to get Stonesgate Farm at Lealholm, which had thirty acres. We were able to keep four cows.'

Cissie and William stayed at Stonesgate for eleven years and worked it painstakingly throughout the First World War. By all the odds, this great conflict should scarcely have touched the isolated pattern of their life. As it was, the front line came right up to their front door on a couple of occasions.

'There were three bombs dropped between our farm and Lealholm side. Nobody got hurt but they broke windows and knocked slates off roofs all over the place. Three big holes were blown out of the moor. I didn't see the planes but I certainly heard them. I suppose they must have been looking for the steelworks up near Middlesbrough. Zeppelins came up the coast, too. And I remember very well when the German fleet bombarded Whitby. I heard this rumbling and I thought it was William pushing a wheelbarrow somewhere but when he came in he told me they had been shelling Whitby. A bit later we went down on the train to see the damage.

'That was a special journey. We didn't get out much and only went to Whitby maybe once a year to get some whisky or gin to sup on pig killing day. The neighbours always came in to help kill the pigs and we'd eat the livers for tea, with warm cakes and a bit to drink afterwards. They were merry times, pig killings. We got a bit of good bacon in those days. You can't now.'

Apart from the odd primitive festival like pig-killing day, life was a relentless round of back-breaking work for Cissie and William. And as Cissie entered her forties in 1918, she fell ill. This should have been the time in her life when the children would normally have been taking some of the work load. But she bore William just one child, which only survived a little time.

'I had two heart attacks and the doctor told us to give up farming. So we left Stonesgate and took a cottage in Lealholm. William went out working on the local farms until there came a time when there was no work and we had to move to East Barnby. In the end, he managed to get a job back on the estate at Mulgrave Castle and he worked there for twenty years until he died. After that, I moved back to Guisborough.

'When I had those heart attacks the doctor put me to bed for seventeen weeks. He said I would never work again. But I must have been taking him in.

'All the others went, one by one and I'm still here, and still doing a bit . . . '

The Phantom Railway

For no apparent reason, a carefully sculpted embankment rises solemnly out of one of Joe Sunley's bottom fields at Grange Farm, Girrick. Underneath the stinging nettles and bushes at the bottom of a nearby gully lies an enormous iron culvert, forty inches in diameter and nearly a hundred feet long.

There are several other baffling pieces of decaying and overgrown engineering which leave a light scar tissue at irregular intervals across the face of East Cleveland. Over an eleven-mile line from Skelton to Glaisdale, which crosses moorland and farming land, there are curious cuttings, giant timbers mouldering under the foliage, small mountains of cinder, more embankments leading to nowhere, rusting iron culverts and at least one open stone culvert, still a tribute to the ancient craft of the stonemason.

It is all part of a phantom railway which might have brought not only prosperity to a land geared economically then as now to the cow byre, but undreamt of wealth. It was officially called the Cleveland Extension Mineral Railway, but swiftly became known as Paddy Waddell's railway under which title it has now passed into local legend. It was to carry a payload of eighty million tons of iron ore said to be deposited under the placid soil on either side of the proposed tracks. Colonel Beaumont's diamond drill said so. This exotic instrument became very excited when it skewered Joe Sunley's land and indicated that each acre now hammered by the hooves of his Cleveland Bays contained twenty thousand tons of ironstone.

The railway was to link with the North Eastern Railway at each end and was sponsored by Joseph Dodds, the Teesdale farm boy who became a great Victorian entrepreneur, a Liberal Member of Parliament and director of many companies. He was powerful enough to insist that the North Eastern ran a direct train between Stockton, his constituency, and London; it was dubbed the Dodds' Express.

The Whitby, Redcar and Middlesbrough Union Railway did not care much for Mr Dodds' running his own railway as well and opposed the idea, but he gained the support and the cash of a group of influential people, including Lord Downe, a large landowner in East Cleveland. The company was capitalised at £170,000 but it is not clear how much public money was raised.

In the autumn of 1874, the first sod was ceremoniously turned on a somewhat remote and inhospitable part of Moorsholm, but several years passed before any serious work was done. And then Paddy Waddell's Irish navvies marched colourfully into East Cleveland.

Paddy Waddell did not actually exist, which is a pity. The man engaged to build the line was a noted Scottish railway engineer of his day called John Waddell, but he did place the day-to-day responsibility of supervising the work with an Irishman. Mr Waddell himself was busy at the time drilling the Mersey Tunnel. The line was dug by muscle and sweat and the clamour of the navvies' work and play echoes through the valleys of the Esk. They lived alongside their work with their women and children and built huts in which to live, which could be moved to keep pace with the work. More than a hundred camped at Girrick for a long time.

This merry, boozing, brawling bunch of men must have revolutionised the gentle social life of the villages through which they sturdily carved their way. The pubs of Lington, Egton, Brotton, Ugthorpe and Newton Mulgrave received brief but glorious bursts of frantic business. Fights were commonplace, and sometimes organised for side stakes.

The builders of the railway were preceded by a glowing prospectus for the company which prophesied that Cleveland was quickly to become 'the greatest steel producing centre in the world' and that Cleveland ironstone would yield about forty-five per cent of metallic iron at about four shillings and sixpence a ton, compared to foreign prices of up to twenty shillings a ton.

'It is difficult to see how any other district will be able to compete with Cleveland in the cost of the production of steel. This new industry will necessarily require the opening of new mines . . . the whole district is alive with schemes for the erection of steel works. There is a deposit of no less than eighty million tons of stone available for working, for which no means of transport can be found until the present line is completed.'

Calculations were made about the returns on a daily traffic of three thousand tons per mile a day and there was confident prose about 'a large revenue expected from the traffic in passengers, live-stock, agricultural produce and the usual mixed traffic of a railway serving an important district in one of the richest counties in England'. Applications were invited for shares offered at par. Ten thousand of them at ten pounds each, but only two pounds called to begin with.

There were certain exaggerations in the prospectus, particularly about the metal yield of the ore, and it seems that the investing public by and large withheld their money. But the navvies' picks and shovels flew in earnest, which means that Mr Waddell must have been confident about being paid. He had promised to finish the job in twenty months.

But twenty years after that first, hopeful spadeful was turned at Moorsholm the line was still not completed. Attempts were made in 1896 to refire the old enthusiasm but as there had been a slump in the price of iron ore and business in general was pretty depressed, it once again came to nought. Even the Glaisdale Ironworks had closed down, leaving behind a mountain of slag and a village full of unemployed.

Poor John Waddell was having great difficulty getting any money out of Cleveland. He was also building the Scarborough to Whitby line, to which he had to extend credit. It was he who constructed the Whitby viaduct. He had been obliged to sell off some of his plant in 1884. Four years later, John Waddell was dead. But the dream of Paddy Waddell's railway lingered on until it came to an official, inglorious end in 1897. John Waddell's heirs applied to the court for the distribution of the deposit paid to Parliament when the Act which approved the construction of the line was first passed. It amounted to a little over eight thousand pounds. The Waddell company must have suffered a stunning loss.

Another grievously disappointed man was a Mr Marsay of Moorsholm. He had obviously considered the business opportunities that Paddy Waddell's railway would bring to Moorsholm and decided to act bravely. On a commanding site in the village, he built the very splendid Railway Hotel . . . two years before the ceremonial sod was turned. It cost him one thousand six hundred pounds, a very substantial sum for 1872, and he got a lot for his money. Bedrooms, a large reception hall and lounge and all the necessary appointments for the entertainment and comfort of the businessmen who were expected to flock to the new mines and steelworks.

Even at this distance in time, it is hard not to feel sorry for the man as he sat in his empty and echoing hotel waiting for the trains that never came. It was a touching act of faith. It took several years to extinguish the flame of hope and then he sadly turned the hotel into the family home, which it remains to this day. At least the Marsays have the satisfaction of living in the most impressive house in Moorsholm.

There is still a chance, however, that the ghosts of Paddy Waddell and Mr Marsay have not yet been laid. In a detailed and scholarly booklet about the railway published by the Whitby Literary and Philosophical Society, the author, Mr R. F. Moore, C.Eng., M.I.E.E., makes the disturbing observation that known reserves of ironstone in the world will be exhausted in about a hundred years. Perhaps it will become necessary to rip the low grade ores from the earth, and no one disputes that East Cleveland squats on an abundance of that. Mr Moors envisages the possibility of a new start to Paddy Waddell's Railway and of the Railway Hotel, Moorsholm, fulfilling its forlorn proprietor's dream.

The World's Biggest Gooseberry

As July slowly ripens into August, a strange fever grips the necklace of villages which adorns the valley of the Esk. Curious arrangements of canvas and wire mesh, some hung with tiny bells, spring up in certain gardens. A deal of furtive prodding around in the soil will be noticed. A sudden summer shower of rain will bring men racing from their cottages carrying umbrellas, which they will hang over bushes. A small squadron of wasps will create near panic.

It all means that the first Tuesday in August is drawing near. That is when the precise weighing instruments will be brought out to decide who is to be the new champion of the Egton Bridge Old Gooseberry Show, the most venerable and celebrated of its kind in the land.

The growing of enormous gooseberries has been going on in the Esk Valley for at least two hundred years. The records of the show at Egton Bridge stretch back that far. It is a deadly serious affair, and nerves are stretched taut in the final run up, for the last few hours in the pre-show life of a potential champion gooseberry are vital. A sudden change in the weather or a hungry insect can ruin months of dedicated work.

Casual visitors to the show who happen to arrive during the weighing-in must feel that they have stumbled on the conclusion of a scientific experiment of the utmost importance. The tension is almost unbearable, as a circle of grey-whiskered old gentlemen peer intently at the scales. An inner circle of judges, spectacles teetering on the ends of their noses, handle tiny weights and gorged fruit with the show precision of diamond merchants. As each class is considered, the yellowing pages of the record books are consulted if a record is in danger of being broken.

Anyone insensitive enough to try and disturb this entranced group before the last, interminable judgement has been solemnly agreed is made mute by a wall of silence.

Only when the entries have been carefully arranged for display on the trestle tables in the church hall can normal life be resumed again.

It is said that the potting sheds of top gooseberry growers are no places for people of delicate constitution. Each one has its dark secrets. It is rumoured that the roots of certain bushes have been nourished with dead rats, dried blood and pungent mixtures of manure personally selected from the moors and farmyards. A well proven bush becomes a family heirloom and is handed down from generation to generation.

There are four hundred species of gooseberry, and four principal colours — green, yellow, red and white. Each has a name, which mostly conjure up visions of whiskered and apoplectic Victorians. Lord Kitchener, Lord Derby and Lloyd George are among the favourite strains. When a bush produces a promising youngster, the post-natal care it receives has to be seen to be believed. Sheets of polythene are stretched out to reflect more heat and tin lids full of water are balanced beneath the lusty young globe to encourage the absorption of more moisture.

A great risk comes from over-cultivation, which can cause the berry to burst like a pricked balloon. A sudden shower on a hot day can make berries pop all through the valley. Sometimes the fruit splits for no apparent reason. Many tragic stories are told of gooseberries, big as young footballs and certain winners, exploding on their way to the show.

Most of the men who compete each year with such passion are elderly. You need to be at least forty before you even begin to develop the craft and patience necessary to nurture champions.

The Egton Bridge show is open to all the world, but the honours generally stay within a few miles of the Esk. The year the cup was taken away as far as Scarborough created as much heartache in the valley as a bad harvest. These men do not take the matter lightly, and the holder of the gooseberry crown is someone to respect. And there is one among them who has become a legend in this land . . . Tom Ventress, the man who grew the biggest gooseberry the world has ever seen.

This feat brought national fame to the Egton Bridge show and Mr Ventress, now in his middle eighties but still a man of vigour and vitality, has basked in the glory ever since his triumph. The show is now heavily featured in the national press each year, and Tom has issued more statements and posed for more photographs than some minor royals. People travel from all over the world to see the show and meet Tom.

The great event occurred in 1952, a superb year for gooseberries. Every grower thought the cup was surely his as aldermanic berries bulged from every bush. But when Tom saw *the* berry bending the branch in his Egton garden, he knew it was the best of a lifetime. In all his years as a consistently successful grower, he had seen nothing like it.

'It was bigger than a golf ball. I was so terrified that a wasp might puncture it that I picked it two days before the show. Then I kept it in a window where a draught would cool it. Too much heat would surely have burst it.'

When that monster, a Transparent, was finally placed on the scales by the judge, a dozen confident competitors froze in disbelief. It weighed in at thirty drams, eight grains — almost two ounces. The champion of champions, the biggest gooseberry ever grown according to official records in which weight is the sole criterion. The previous record, held by a London Red, had stood for exactly one hundred years.

'And it weighed *more* than two ounces when I picked it,' claims Tom.

The immortal fruit was reverently photographed for posterity and Tom received many requests from several countries for cuttings off the proud mother bush — and for advice.

'I just prune hard and use good farm manure,' he says — with the canny look of the typical Eskdalian, never so daft as to give away all his secrets.

Like his friend, the late George Harland of Glaisdale (another keen gooseberry grower, who took the championship one year), Tom Ventress is a Dalesman with a deep interest in local history. He has a sparkling memory and possesses an absorbing scrapbook which dates back to pre-1914.

Tom was born in 1892, the son of an ironstone miner who worked at Liverton, near Loftus. The Boer War was at its height when Tom was a lad and he retains vivid memories of the fervour it aroused in East Cleveland.

'They used to go mad round there when something happened. There were torchlight processions through the streets and big bonfires for Mafeking, Ladysmith . . . or whenever there was a change in the fortunes of the war. It was amazing the way they carried on.'

But life at home was not too happy for Tom and his sister. The strain of mining made his father irritable and prone to bouts of drinking. And his mother became ill.

'Mother had my sister, Mary, sixteen months after I was born and she was never right again. She died when she was thirty-two and I was ten. My Dad got a housekeeper but eight months later the mine stopped, so I was sent with Mary to live with my grandparents in Goathland. And they were in their eighties! I can clearly recall the day we were taken to them. It was the twenty-first of January 1902, and there was a slight griming of snow as our horse and trap came over Jolly Sailor bank. By the end of the next day whole flocks of sheep were buried in the snow, and they stayed buried for six weeks. When it cleared they were still alive but they wobbled about all over the place.'

Despite their age, Tom's grandparents were extremely active farmers and brought up Tom and his sister with affection; but there were hardships.

'No old age pension in those days. A quarter pound of butter had to last all week and we never saw a roast joint from one year end to another. But there were plenty of pigs being killed in the neighbourhood so we always had a bit of bacon. My grandfather used to go off to work with a big lump of plain cake and a piece of fat bacon and he was as happy as a king.'

Tom's grandfather went on to live until his one hundredth and first year. He was the huntsman for both the Goathland and Staintondale Hunts in his time. At ninety-three, he attended the first meet of the Egton Hunt. Tom's grandmother was another remarkable old person.

'She fell ill once and they sent for the doctor, who came two miles on horseback to see her. After he examined her he said "Sorry, I can do nowt for her. She's like a clock that's run down."

'So we thought she was going to die. She lay in bed for three weeks, just taking a bit of gruel and a drop of whisky. My grandfather used to go each Friday to the store and to the butcher for a bit of houndsmeat, and as he was going one week he said "Is there owt I can bring you, Mother?" She replied "Bring me a pair of new slippers, and I might get up." So he did, and she got up and lived for another five years, until she was ninetythree.'

As Tom grew up, his father was lodging in various parts of East Cleveland. And then he remarried, to the landlady of the Horse Shoe Inn at Egton, which had an adjoining farm of eighty acres. The new landlord knew nothing about farming but his son, now fifteen, did. So he was summoned.

'I worked for him with no wage until I was twenty-two. If I hadn't had to work as an ostler at the pub as well I would never have had any money at all. They used to charge sixpence to take a horse in and I would get a copper or two for myself.

'Businessmen from Whitby used to come out to Egton in their traps on a Sunday and have a whisky or two, and I did well out of that. Whenever one particular man came I'd stand with his horse even if it was knee-deep in snow because he always gave me a bob. Do you know, I saved eighty pounds over the years that way.'

And then came 1912, the memory of which can still send a shudder through the old men of the Esk. Tom Ventress talks about it in hushed tones, even now.

'1912 was a disaster. The worst year anyone can remember. The crops failed, the hay was all bad and there was nothing to feed the horses and cattle. My father made me go out with a cart and three horses every day, to take five tons of road metal five times a day between Egton and Grosmont. We only got thirteen and ninepence for doing it, but it bought a bag of oats which helped to keep the stock alive. If there had been two years like 1912 there would have been no farmers left round here. As it was, some of the young men emigrated to Australia.'

Shortage of money did not stop Tom from becoming a lady's man around Egton for he grew into a handsome lad with a dashing moustache. He attended the pig killings, threshing days and other festivities and enjoyed 'Martinmas madness' to the full. A lot of his pals were at farm place, returning home only at Martinmas for a week's holiday. They made the most of it.

'Nobody went to bed that week at all,' recalls Tom. 'It was one big party. It was the only time of the year that the lads at farm place could really let rip, and their parents didn't mind because they were so pleased to see them home again. They'd bring out the home-made beer and lemonade and let us get on with it. There was plenty to eat, too. Real good food, all home-made.

'During the day we'd play cricket, football and have wrestling matches, and at night we went to someone's house. Everything was turned into a big event—if someone's cow was due to calve we'd all sit round in the byre playing cards until it arrived.

'The girls would join in the parties, too, because it was the time to find a sweetheart or renew the romance which had been started last Martinmas. It was during Martinmas that I began to court my wife.'

Tom's particular pals were the Hodgson boys of East End Farm, Egton, and he never missed their party. They had a sister called Flora . . .

'I didn't pay much attention to her and then she got engaged to a lad who went off to fight in the First World War. But one day I went up to their farm to help with the threshing and Flora was waiting on the men in the stack yard. Now the man who was running the threshing machine was a devil among women, and I knew that. He was always boasting and I overheard him saying that he was going to take her for a walk that night. So I said "You bloody won't, if I have owt to do with it." Well, when we sat down to play cards that night he was so damned uneasy that I managed to persuade her to sit down and play with us. By gum, it did set him against me.'

Tom's new-found interest in Flora was not welcome in the Hodgson household at first because her betrothed was a comparatively wealthy young man. Tom would have to improve his position in life.

'I got on to my father and played hell with him. I told him I must have some money because I wanted to get married but he just turned round and said: "If you're not satisfied then find another job." But my stepmother heard about it and said she would let me have eight shillings a week.'

Tom tried to land a job as a representative for a Darlington firm but just failed because he was so young.

'Flora had broken off her engagement but even so I had to tell her that it didn't look as though I'd be in a position to marry her for many years. And my father was being as awkward as ever he could be, spending time in the pub when he should have been working with me. When my stepmother died and he married again within the year

I found it very difficult to get my money off him—still eight bob a week—and sometimes I went as long as seventeen weeks without wage. And then he wouldn't give it to me himself . . . I'd find it left in the corn bin or somewhere.

'Then one day I met a director of the firm I'd applied to, and he told me that I only needed to try again and I'd get a job. I was twenty-six at the time, and I said I'd think about it. Soon after, my father turned up for work in the turnip field at ten past twelve—time to be going back for dinner, not start work. I was so disgusted that I threw my hoe up the field and went inside and wrote a letter for that job.'

And so, two years later at St Hilda's Church, Egton, Thomas William Ventress, local agent for Messrs Ord and Maddison, Ltd, married his patient sweetheart. His father did not attend the wedding. But by now Tom could afford a honeymoon.

Tom and Flora raised three sons and two daughters and when they celebrated their golden wedding in 1970 they had thirteen grandchildren and six great-grandchildren. It was also Gooseberry Show Day, and Tom rounded off a splendid occasion by looming large in the prize list for the twenty-third successive year.

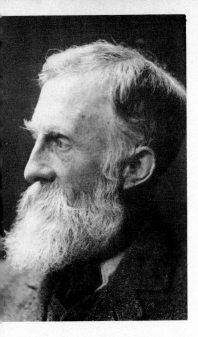

THE MISSING ART OF TOM WATSON: Left: Frank Meadow Sutcliffe (The Sutcliffe Gallery). **Right: A self-portrait of Tom Watson towards the end of his life.**

An early study of Whitby harbour by Frank Meadow Sutcliffe.

Above and opposite, top: Pictures by Frank Meadow Sutcliffe (The Sutcliffe Gallery).

Opposite, bottom: A family birthday party with Tom at the head of the table. Picture by Tom Watson.

CHILDREN OF ESKDALE: Above: The Raw family of Lawns-gate Farm, Fryup. John and Dot are in the centre, with their children Susan, Shirley, David, Christine and Alan.

Opposite: Father and son return from a hunting trip.

PRINCE: Above: Alan Raw and Prince.

Opposite: The Raws and Prince. The lower photograph also includes the author of this book (centre back).

Alan Raw inside the helicopter used in the filming of 'The Children of Eskdale'.

Alan helping with the filming.

A Very Special Dalesman

When Aunt Cissie's father was laboriously tilling the soil of Oakley Walls Farm at Lealholm behind his old grey mare, his plough must often have struck sparks off some curious sandstone slabs in one of the fields. Half a century later one of George Raw Readman's successors at Oakley Walls dug a little deeper with the ploughshare and turned over one of the slabs. Underneath was part of a human skull.

The farmer and the friends he brought to view this phenomenon knew exactly what to do about it—send for George Harland of Glaisdale.

George Harland was a very special kind of Dalesman. He had lived and worked in Glaisdale for all but one of his eighty-seven years, first as a farm lad when he left school at thirteen and then as a stonemason. Inspired by the beauty and the folklore all around him, he became a self-taught historian, naturalist and archaeologist of real importance, widely admired by the recognised academics in these subjects.

George instantly realised, for instance, that the stone slabs ploughed up at Oakley Walls formed an early Stone Age Kist grave. He knew its rarity and importance and swiftly arranged for the acknowledged experts to come and see and verify. Those slabs and remains are now in a museum.

Delving into the past was an obsession with George and he became a familiar sight in the neighbourhood as he dug around the known and suspected sites of primitive habitation and industry in the Dale and patiently tracked down and analysed old church registers, deeds and other yellowing documents. He was responsible for proving that between 1557 and 1743 Glaisdale was a thriving woollen area with two busy mills—'the Bradford of the Dales'. He was also deeply interested in the traces of early ironstone mining in the Egton area which some historians believed was the site of a Brigante village until it was proved that the holes in the ground were not homes at all, but pits left by iron ore miners of Roman times. George drew a full section and plan of these workings for posterity, before they were eventually ploughed in.

George had a keen eye for the fascinating minutiae of rural life and a ready ear for any folklore and—most important of all—he recognised that it was worth recording. He was also fascinated by the old rites and customs of the Dale which had survived into his childhood and before he died in 1969, wrote down his memories and the details of his research. The rest of his story is taken from these notes.

George Harland was born in 1882, at Sleights, near Whitby, the son of a foreman quarryworker. His father moved to Glaisdale before George's first birthday. He and his four brothers and four sisters went to school in the High Street. Fees were paid on Monday morning and ranged from three-half-pence to fourpence, quite a burden for a large family.

'School was just one large room with a door on one side for the girls and one on the opposite side for the boys. There was no porch or cloakroom. The walls of the room were very damp and drops of moisture stood like peas on the walls when the weather was muggy. The only heating was a stove in the centre of the room, with a smoke pipe going out of the roof. One very cold winter the master used to march us round the room in single file every fifteen or twenty minutes to keep us warm.

'Strict silence was observed in the school; only the master's voice could be heard or a scholar reading aloud. There were always two sticks on the master's deck which he bought at a little shop close to the school. The cane for the boys cost twopence and the one for the girls a penny. Old John Breckon, who owned the shop, did a rattling good trade with his sticks and always had a bundle in stock. When any of us had done anything wrong there was a saying "Thou'll get twopenny for that".

'Twice in my schooldays the pupils ran away at dinner time on Royal Oak Day, the 29th May. The first time I was too young to take part, but I remember seeing them off. Two tall girls each held a corner of an old bed-sheet, which was blowing in the wind, with the rest of the scholars running either underneath it or following close behind. They were shouting the old saying: "Royal Oak Day, if you don't give us a holiday we'll run away".

'They were tough times, especially for cottagers. Many of them had large families. In the street where I lived there were two families with twelve children each, and it was quite general to have eight or nine children in a family. A labourer's wage was eighteen shillings a week, if they worked full time. Of course, this would be much reduced in bad weather. Some mothers took in washing and others went out to work to help. There was a lot of firewood carried out of Arncliffe and Limber woods. It was a common sight to see five or six mothers with some of their children emerging from the wood carrying sticks on a fine summer's evening. They were not allowed to use axes or saws.

'The very poor and old people who were unable to work would get two shillings or two and six per week. The Registrar from the

Board of Guardians came round on horseback to pay it.

'Food in those days was very cheap. Even so it's a mystery to me how our parents kept us fed and clothed. Eggs in the summertime were generally sixteen or twenty a shilling. Butter was eightpence a pound, shoulder of bacon sixpence a pound. An excellent dinner could be made with sixpenny-worth of cuttings from the butcher. There was usually a fair amount of liver, sweetbreads, bits of beef, and so on. The cattle in those days were often fat, and suet could be bought very cheaply and was sometimes given away.

'There were three grocers in the village. Two of these employed an apprentice who always had plenty of work to do, for nearly everything was weighed out in the shop. There was very little packaged stuff, only soap and blacking for shoes and black lead for polishing firesides and ovens. A machine was used for cleaning the currants and another one for grinding the coffee. The shelves were packed with large canisters about two feet high and fifteen inches in diameter, which were marked with the groceries they contained. Three different kinds of flour were always kept in stock. There was also a drum of treacle which had a lever tap attached. Treacle was then twopence a pound. The groceries were delivered to the farms in spring carts.

'The farmers in those days were chiefly tenant farmers on different estates and often had to sell their stock to pay the rent for a lot of them lived from hand to mouth. Many horses were reared, chiefly heavy working cart horses.

'On some estates if farmers wanted to plough an extra field, they would first have to get permission from the landlord or his agent. Most landlords reared large quantities of game which did a lot of damage to crops. Even rabbits and hares were protected until Mr Gladstone passed the Hares and Rabbits Bill.

'Seed was dressed with wine and a little lime to give it a good start and some protection from the birds. Sparrows were a menace and the farmer shot as many as possible. They used to lay a long trail of grain and then hide with a gun and fire along the line. They would get fifteen or even twenty birds with one shot. One farmer told his neighbour that he had caught twenty-three. His neighbour said: "Most I ivver got with one shot, was ninety-nine." "Thou might as well have said a hundred," his friend replied. "Noo a'm nut going to lee just for one sparrow."

George Harland was passionately interested in music and played an enthusiastic double bass in the Glaisdale String Orchestra for many years. A brass band also thrived in the village and played at the festivities at Danby when Lord Downe returned from the Zulu wars.

The string orchestra was open to both sexes and this continually led to total chaos at one of the leading engagements of the year — playing round the Dale at Christmas. Curiously, many of the younger, attractive ladies would have trouble with their violins.

Strings would break like cotton. In each case, a young man would offer to help the hapless maid and both were left behind to mend the instrument. They were rarely seen again and the night would finish up with a handful of older men and women trying to cope.

Some of those musical romances went all the way to the altar, and weddings in Glaisdale turned into a festival shared by all the village. Just about everybody was a guest. George Harland had warm memories:

'After the service and wedding feast the guests would congregate in a field, near the local public house. Foot races would be run with prizes such as a silk handkerchief for the ladies or a tie or tobacco for the men. The competitors were often in their stockinged feet. After that they would gather in the pub where usually two shillings and sixpence or five shillings was placed on a plate and then handed round for the guests to add to. This was always done with two plates, one on the top of the other. Money placed on the top plate was tipped on to the one beneath so no one knew how much anyone else had given. The total was then given to the landlord for beer for the company. It was served in half-gallon jugs. Pots of hot ale sweetened and spiced were brought out of houses along the route from the church after the wedding ceremony and offered to the bride and groom. As many as twelve of these hot pots were offered in the distance of one mile at a wedding I once attended.

'The brideswain custom was still held when I was a small boy. A carriage loaded with household goods travelled from the bride's father's house to the bridegroom's. A great parade was seen on these occasions. The wagon or carriage was drawn by oxen garlanded with ribbons, while a young woman sat at a spinning wheel in the centre of the load and the friends of the parties increased the gifts as the procession went on.

'I well remember a song that used to be sung in the pubs at these wedding parties. Everyone would be given a tot of ale and the company would sing:

> The bride's good health is now beginning,
> In spite of the Turk or the Spanish King.
> The groom's good health we'll not let pass,
> We'll have them both into one glass.
> See See See that he drinks it all,
> See See See that he lets none fall,
> For if he does he shall have two
> And so shall the company all.'

During his retirement, George Harland devoted much of his time to building up a fascinating dossier on the history and archaeology of his Dale. He was constantly in demand as a speaker and became one of the best known and most respected men in East Cleveland.

The Ballad of Beggar's Bridge

The most romantic bridge in all the Yorkshire Dales is the narrow, picturesque stone arch which spans the Esk at Glaisdale. It is called Beggar's Bridge and round it is woven a touching legend of true love.

In the sixteenth century, a farm lad from Egton called Tom Ferris lost his heart to a Glaisdale lass, Agnes Richardson. It is said they met at St Hilda's Fair at Whitby and danced the night away together. But Tom was only the son of a poor farmer and Agnes the daughter of the Squire of Glaisdale, who announced that he had no intention of allowing her to throw herself away on 'a beggar'. The starry-eyed Agnes defied him and left a lighted candle at her window whenever her father was out of the house. Tom would come leaping over the stepping stones across the Esk to swear his undying love.

Tom realised that he would have to change his status in life to win over the stern Squire and decided to seek his fortune on the high seas. He signed on as a member of the crew of a ship about to join with Drake to meet the Spanish Armada.

The night before he was due to sail, Tom set off for Glaisdale to say farewell to his love. But when he reached the banks of the Esk he found the river was in flood. The stepping stones were well under water. He tried to swim across but was beaten back by the torrent. Bitterly, he returned to Whitby and as his ship slipped out of Whitby Bay and trimmed sail for the English Channel and glory, he vowed that should fame and fortune ever come his way he would build a bridge over the Esk at Glaisdale.

So runs the legend. What cannot be denied is that Tom and Agnes were real people and Tom became rich and famous. There is a portrait of him in Trinity House, Hull. It seems Tom took to sea-faring with a will and buccaneered with great profit against the Spaniards. He returned in triumph to Glaisdale to thumb his nose at the Squire and carry off the faithful Agnes. They are believed to have married in the local Chapel of Ease at Glaisdale.

The bridge was duly built at Tom's expense and went on in later years to have less fortunate associations. It became the scene of several celebrated accidents, all involving horses. George Harland records three incidents which took place in his lifetime. First a farm foreman went over the side with his cart, one ton of basic slag, one

93

ton of coping stones and three horses. The horses survived and the only injury sustained by the foreman was a broken collar bone. A few years later they were followed by a coachman and a carriage and pair, all of whom escaped serious injury. But the last and most spectacular accident occurred when two horses drawing a carrier's wagon inexplicably leapt over the side. The leading horse escaped, but the other hung itself, and dangled there gruesomely as the villagers pondered how to retrieve the body. A local photographer, thought to be a Mr Readman, managed to get to the scene and assemble his equipment in time to take a memorable picture.

Tom Ferris, who became Lord Mayor of Hull, lavished more generosity on Glaisdale and other places, endowing churches and aiding orphans before he died in 1631. Trinity House, Hull, over which he presided three times as Warden, presented a superb silver communion service in his name to Glaisdale Church. But the best memorial to the love story of Thomas and Agnes is Beggar's Bridge itself.

The Missing Art of Tom Watson

As Frank Meadow Sutcliffe was busy with his camera among the old fishermen, tall-masted ships and naked urchins of Whitby harbour, another pioneer photographer was pedalling an enormously laden Rudge-Whitworth bicycle along the lanes of the Esk valley. His name was Tom Watson.

Frank Sutcliffe collected over sixty awards from many countries for his work; Tom Watson did not enter any of his. Yet he worked the same area as Sutcliffe for three-quarters of a century, and when he died at ninety-four in 1957 he left behind approximately three tons of plates. Those of local interest lie uncatalogued in Whitby Museum, whilst an industry grows around the Sutcliffe plates. Books are published about Sutcliffe's life and work; he has become fashionable in the salons of New York; and a batch of prints made personally by the master reached an astronomical sum at a recent auction. The man himself died long before his work became so valuable, in 1941 when he was ninety-one.

It is only partly true to say that Tom Watson suffered by living in the shade of the immortal Sutcliffe, because he did not compete in the same artistic field. Sutcliffe, who came from the middle class, was deliberately creative, taking great care about composition and the arrangement of his subjects and experimenting with the use of light. He even tried shooting against the light, one of the first photographers to succeed with this daring technique. Watson was an artisan by class, and most unadventurous in his photography. And yet . . .

His living depended on postcards and those formally arranged sepia groups so loved by the Victorians (which, nevertheless, speak volumes about the attitudes of the day), and so he took what he was told to take. But there is clear evidence to suggest that a photographer of real importance, maybe even outstanding artistry, lurked beneath the surface.

Tom Watson was the son of the head joiner at Mulgrave Castle, home of the Lords Normanby in Lythe. He was apprenticed to his father but as soon as he came 'out of his time' promptly left for London and a polytechnic college where he studied photography for five years.

On his return home he set up business in Lythe, where he was appointed court photographer to the Normanbys. All their weddings, births and other events of significance were dutifully recorded by Tom throughout his career. That collection must have some importance. But Tom Watson also had another separate life, when all the restrictions imposed on his artistry by the necessity of earning a living could be cast aside. During the twenty years before the twentieth century dawned he travelled regularly throughout Europe, and made one visit to America. With him went his cameras *and* a portable dark room. His trip to America at the end of the last century took in the World's Fair at Chicago, New York and other cities in the United States and Canada. He climbed the mountains of Switzerland, tottering across glaciers with his equipment, and set up his tripod in the fields and vineyards of southern France among the peasants and oxen-drawn carts.

His sole surviving child, William Watson, now retired and living in Whitby, remembers these photographs vividly.

'My father had several albums full of pictures taken on his travels abroad. He used to show them to me when I was a child and tell me about the places he had visited. He was very impressed by the World's Fair and took a lot of the machinery and stands on view. There were street scenes in various cities, he went to Niagara Falls and took shots there of the Royal Canadian Mounted Police.

'I remember one he took of himself in Switzerland crossing a glacier with a black peaked cap on his head and a handkerchief round the back of his neck to protect it against the sun. The pictures were more artistic than the general ones he took, particularly those in the vineyards of France, which lent themselves to creative work.

'There were hundreds of them, and all in sepia.'

Tom Watson may have travelled Europe with Jules Verne, for his son remembers being shown the complete works of Verne, all signed by the author.

'Father said that he was a distant cousin and talked as though he knew him.'

When he became a family man, Tom Watson's travels were undertaken mostly in East Cleveland. His bicycle was hung with his camera, slides and tripod in specially designed cases.

'When he died,' Tom's son says, 'I found about three tons of plates in the studio. I had no place to keep that amount of glass and I knew the museum people had taken what they wanted so I called in a scrap merchant. He gave me five pounds for the plates and the props in the studio and took them away. The larger plates were washed clean and sold for greenhouse glass, and the others destroyed. I suppose those he took on his early travels would be among them.

'But the albums of American and European prints have vanished.

So have the signed copies of Jules Verne.'

Perhaps they are lying forgotten in some cupboard in Whitby. Unless those missing albums turn up one day, the world will never know just how good a photographer Tom Watson really was.

Children of Eskdale

The Yorkshire Dales have two populations. The minority who live there and the majority who surge like a tidal wave through the valleys at the weekend.

Perhaps they are responding to the same call which made Ruth Kitching exchange her barrister's wig and gown for wellington boots and an old coat tied with string. Perhaps they know instinctively they are swimming in an alien sea. Certainly the Sunleys, the Welfords and their kind, those whose forbears did not flee the land for the loom, do not have their emotions mauled every fine weekend. They know a serenity which is special to those who stayed and suffered with the land. And a few fortunate people have reaped such a reward from this loyalty and their happiness is so complete, that it hurts the soul.

Such people are the Raws, the true Children of Eskdale.

John Raw is the head of the family and the eighth of his line to farm the stubborn soil of Eskdale. He was also born into a Cleveland sub-aristocracy too subtle to be readily detected. Like his father before him, he is a kind of yeoman patrician, more of a natural leader of his community than any of the loftily titled men in their proud mansions. His wife, Dorothy, a child of the same land and traditions, seems to have been ordained to help him perpetuate the Raw line. This she has done with a rare beauty, giving him five of the fairest and most fortunate children in this island.

The life that the Raws lead from their farm perched prettily on the edge of the vast sweep of Fryup Dale is so well balanced, healthy and free from most twentieth-century pressures that it is almost impossible to find a rift in the lute. They enjoy all the benefits of progress but have not had to accept any of its disadvantages, or in any way damage their rural harmony. They have enough money to afford a car and a telephone, but not enough to overheat their ambitions or lure them from their natural environment. They enjoy a social life rich in variety and share it with the people with whom they were raised. The five young Raws, ablaze with the lusty joys of living on a farm, have all the sophistication endowed by modern communications and are being educated as well as, if not better than, most city children. But they do not suffer from pollution, motorways, urban claustrophobia, high-rise flats or the screech of industry. And they can go out into the night alone without fear.

The children's essential points of reference remain the same as their father's and those of his father before him. From the commanding heights of his farm, John Raw can overlook the valley which has nourished his ancestors over the centuries. Ajalon House in Fryup Dale has been the mute witness of the life and death, joys and disasters of eight generations of Raws. John Raw was born there in 1933, one of eight children.

His father, Frank Raw, a clever and successful farmer, carried much stature in the community. He was appointed by Lord Downe and other landowners to act as their agent, and the Government made him an Agricultural Executive Officer during the last war. He was also a probate valuer.

There was no hardship in John Raw's childhood, just hard work and a lot of fun. School was a mile and a quarter across the fields, there was a stable full of horses to ride, a river to swim in and plenty of companionship.

'They were happy days. We didn't stray far from the Dale but we didn't need to because there was such a strong community sense. A lot of the activities such as threshing day, sheep shearing and the like were shared. Everyone used to come and help on those occasions.'

A steam-driven threshing machine toured the area visiting each farm, possibly the same one (now powered by a tractor) which America Jack Welford still hires. Frank Raw would buy half a ton of coal for every day he required its services and his sons would steel themselves for days of intense labour.

'It was traditional for a farmer's son to carry water for the machine and they were always given a day off from school for this purpose. That thing swallowed hundreds of gallons and we used to carry buckets literally all day to an old poss tub at the side of it. In the old days when we grew sixteen to twenty acres of corn it used to go on for three days, but later we could do it in one day.

'Sheep shearing days were much more enjoyable. We always clipped the last Saturday in June—by hand—and all the family, neighbours and their wives and children used to come for that. We used to shear all the lambs before dinner, just taking their breast wool off, and do the sheep in the afternoon. We children had to catch the sheep, sometimes three or four hundred of them, and carry away the fleeces. The shearing was done in a cow byre and we had to drive them into the adjoining byre. It was great fun at first because we'd do a bit of sheep riding, falling off and the like. By the middle of the afternoon it became a real labour dragging those sheep around, but you still had it to do.

'Then when it was all over the men used to play quoits and go for a farm walk. That's an old custom which has nearly died out now, but whenever there was an occasion there would be a farm walk to inspect the buildings and the stock. The children would play hide and seek and then cricket with the older youths before going in for a big tea party. I always looked forward to sheep shearing when I was a lad.

'Pig killing was a big day too. The last one I remember at Ajalon, we killed seventeen pigs. My father was an expert at that, and it was in the days before you had to be licensed to kill a pig. He had a wooden mallet and an iron punch which worked exactly the same way as a humane killer, placing the punch on the pig's head and driving it home with the mallet instead of a cartridge. Then the pig's throat would be cut and blood caught in a trough to be made into black puddings. Whilst this was going on the women would be boiling a large copper full of water for the scalding. Great pride was taken in the copper and it was kept highly polished. The boiling water was poured off over the pig to scald the hair and the skin off before it was dressed, which was another job in which much pride was taken. There would be another big tea and then it was traditional for all the men to play nap for small stakes until a very late hour, and there would be a bit to drink. On some farms they would play right through until daybreak. Myself, I didn't like pig killing very much when I was young probably because of all the blood. I know one of my younger brothers wouldn't go anywhere near, so my father didn't bother us until we were old enough to be useful. Later on, I used to kill my own pigs in exactly the same way. Now we take them down to the slaughterhouse, although I still bring them back home for curing.'

The primitive glory of this kind of rural life, cementing together a community which had thrived for many centuries in the Yorkshire Dales, had its final flourish when John Raw was growing to manhood in the nineteen-forties and 'fifties. Apart from a few tenacious pockets, it is now but a warm memory and the valleys are the poorer for its passing.

There were so many highdays in the young life of John Raw that some of the more widely accepted anniversaries were discarded. Birthdays, for instance.

'They used to come and go without anyone really noticing. I never used to get any presents. Except one, that is. I was walking to school with my sister on one birthday during the war when she offered to carry my gasmask to mark the occasion. That's the only birthday present I can remember getting, when I was young. Mind you, two days after Frank and I became twenty-one my father had his sixtieth birthday, and we cracked a bottle of whisky for that.'

Before and after school John helped milk twelve cows by hand whilst his twin shared the shepherding of around three hundred sheep up on Glaisdale high moor. There were always three pairs of work horses, mainly shires, and a stag (young horse) in the stables. Every spring one or two young horses were broken on the Raw spread.

'We had two riding horses as well, one a halfbred Cleveland Bay called Jess and a thoroughbred gelding called Sam. We practically lived on horseback in those days, riding them up to the moor to take feed to the sheep or going errands down to the village. My father rode with the Glaisdale Hunt and always kept a couple of hounds for them.

'I suppose we were well off by local standards. Later on, we even had a car, one of the first in the Dale.'

Three miles across the sheep tracks of the high moor from Ajalon House lies the village of Glaisdale. It was there at Number 10 High Street, on New Year's Day in 1938, as the hounds bayed and hare soup was served to mark the first hunt of the year, that Dorothy was born, the first child of William and Annie Welford.

At that time, William Welford — a distant relative of those other Welfords at America House — earned a living filling tubs full of hard slag, which were then taken away by Surrey County Council to make their roads. The blast furnace for local iron ore which had once flourished at Glaisdale had waned and died with Paddy Waddell's railway, which was supposed to link it with the major industrial centres of the North East, but the legacy of its waste gave work to another generation.

By a strange quirk of nature the slag heaps also gave people an exotic fruit for their tables — wild strawberries. Dot Raw remembers them growing profusely on the arid slopes, and she and her brother and sister used to collect jam jars full of the tiny berries in the summers of their childhood.

Like her husband, Dot has glowing memories of a kind of young life which has now virtually disappeared, when children created their own fun out in the open.

'We played all the old games in the streets of Glaisdale — ball games, hop scotch on the pavement, cowboys and indians. It was quite the thing at weekends for all the mothers to take their children down to Mill Wood for a picnic and we used to swim in the River Esk. It was very clean and safe, as long as we didn't go near a place which had a whirlpool. There had been a few tragedies because of that, I believe. We never had much money, but it didn't matter. We were all well fed and clothed. Occasionally, my father used to take us on the train to Whitby for a treat and there was the annual Sunday School outing to Scarborough. But we didn't go far very often, because we didn't have a car, and we never had a family holiday.'

Dot changed her home several times as a child because her father, the son of a farmer, went back to the land. After taking one or two positions, he settled at Wind Hill, a farm in between Glaisdale and Lealholm.

'I was about thirteen at the time and Wind Hill was bought by a

101

man called Stonehouse, who had been a tea planter in India. He left when the British got out of India, and was the talk of the village because he paid what was then a fantastic price for a ninety-odd acre farm — five thousand pounds. (He was a bachelor at the time and very kind, although he was very remote and rarely mixed with the villagers. He never talked about his past.) He learned how to be a farmer from books and hired my father to help him. The wage included our services too. We lived at one end of the long farmhouse and had to help on the farm and look after him. Mum and I had to cook his meals and keep the house clean, including the dusting of the elephant's tusks and other trophies from India.

'There was always a lot of work — and work came first. I looked after the calves, and I remember getting ring worms from them once, all across my chest. The ironing was always waiting for me when I came home from school on Monday evening.'

When Dot, a bright and extroverted young lady, left school at sixteen, she managed to avoid a shop counter job and found an outlet for her creative ability by persuading photographer Bill Eglan Shaw to hire her. He is now well established in Whitby as the custodian of the world-famous Frank Meadow Sutcliffe plates, which he promotes and markets with energy and flair. At the time Dot joined him he was in a more modest way of business in the village of Loftus, twelve miles away from Wind Hill.

'I had to take lodgings in the village because there was no bus service in the area at the time. That took thirty shillings out of my wages, which were only two pounds. I used to spend most of my time in the dark room doing the printing and finishing and went out with Mr Shaw on weddings and commercial work as his assistant.'

Two or three years before she went to work, Dot had become aware of a farm lad from over the moor with a mass of dark, wavy hair and a permanent grin. He too had cast a reflective eye on the girl with long pigtails known through the dale as 'Little Dot' because she was so small, although she had 'plenty to say for herself'.

The Welfords and the Raws knew each other because Dot's father was known everywhere as 'Warag Willie'. He had an appointment under the war agricultural administration and ran the thresher which attended Ajalon House each year.

'We really met first of all at the cricket matches between Glaisdale and Fryup,' Dot recalls. 'Then he took me home from the Glaisdale village dance — in his car! He was able to cut a real dash in those days because he could borrow his father's car, but on the other hand he couldn't dance and there were fourteen others in the car as well. Then he got called up to do his National Service and he asked me to write to him. It wasn't serious then because I was only fourteen and he was eighteen, but it was quite something to have a soldier's photograph on your dressing-table. I had lots of other boyfriends as well.'

Already, John Raw stood out from the other young men of the Dale. They turned naturally to him for leadership, as their fathers had turned to his father, and by sixteen he was the chairman of the local Young Farmers' Club.

The sons of farmers were almost exclusively exempt from National Service but John, who admits he wanted to go anyway, was trapped by two things: his honesty, and the fact that he was a twin.

'When my brother Frank and I went for an interview he put himself down as a shepherd, which he was, and I put myself down as a stocksman, which was also true because we were a stock-rearing farm. Then this woman sat behind the desk asked casually whether I did anything else but look after the stock, and I said "Oh yes." Well, that did it. She promptly said she would have to classify me as a general farmworker and no arguments, which meant I wasn't exempt. Frank was all right because he worked solely with stock — although there couldn't really have been a farmer's son anywhere who specialised in one job.

'I went in on the day that King George died and we had to be on parade for his funeral three days later. That transformation from being a farm lad to a well-drilled and licked-into-shape soldier on a parade ground was one of the big traumas of my life.

'But then it all changed again and became two years of sheer luxury. I joined the Royal Artillery and my unit was sent to Germany, which I enjoyed very much. Suddenly it dawned on me that there was something else in the world apart from farming and Fryup Dale. I'm afraid I began to like the freedom and the wide horizons of life on the continent. I really took to it. And I began to fear coming back to farming when the time drew near for demob. In fact, I very nearly emigrated to South Africa. I got to know a major who was tied up with gold mining and goodness knows how many other things out there, and he tried very hard to persuade me to go.'

But there was a pull of the diminutive girl now rising sixteen, with the raven hair and large brown eyes, who kept his photograph in her bedroom and wrote romantic letters.

'I don't suppose you could say we were really serious about each other, in spite of those letters,' says Dot. 'He used to send me nylons though, sheer black nylons with seams. You just couldn't buy them in England at the time and he used to swap coffee for them. I was the envy of all the girls in the Dale.

'But oh dear, he was terribly unsettled when he first came out of the army. It lasted for a full year. If there was a fight going then he would be in it.'

'Yes, I suppose I was a bit of a lad when I came out of the army,' admits John. 'But I was under quite a bit of strain trying to adjust to living in a Dale again and wondering whether I should get out of farming — out of the country, perhaps. So I used to go

103

around with my pals, having a few pints — not many, because we were still hard up — and looking for a bit of excitement.'

One of the places guaranteed to provide the excitement they craved was the fishing village of Staithes, a steep place full of quaint alleys and crooked houses which looks as though it has been stolen from Cornwall. Generations of youths have clashed along its moonlit harbour and cobbled streets, for Staithes has always been the traditional flashpoint between the two religions of East Cleveland — the sea dwellers' and the dalesfolk's. 'Tater-heads' and 'scaly-backs' are the insults traditionally traded between the two factions, and the dalesfolk have sometimes been driven out of Staithes in a shower of fish heads. There is still said to be tension between the two groups in the senior playgrounds in the Whitby area.

Throughout this turbulent period in John's life, Dot never strayed from his side. Gradually, John began to direct more of his energies back into farming but he had no wages or set pocket money. This came hard to a man used to regular pay.

'I never really knew what my wages were. Father used to put them straight into the bank in a lump sum once or twice a year. I had to make most of my pocket money by trapping and shooting rabbits to sell to a man who used to come round the Dale. I'd get a bit of cash sometimes on a Saturday night by getting round my mum but I often had to count coppers to see if I had enough for both a pint and a ticket to the dance. But Dad was very good to me when I came out of the army, allowing me to use the car quite a bit. And then one day he came to me and said: "You had to go away when your brothers stayed at home earning wages so I'm going to give you Sam. There's quite a keen buyer for him."'

Encouraged, John threw himself into the social life of the Dale, hunting with the Glaisdale and becoming chairman of the cricket club (which he remains to this day). Then his father went into hospital for two major operations so he had to shoulder even more responsibility on the farm. At the same time Dot's father had to move to another job on a farm twenty miles away at Nunthorpe, near Middlesbrough. The ex-tea planter had decided to stop farming Wind Hill. But this did not dampen John's ardour.

'He used to come three times a week, Wednesdays, Saturdays, and Sundays,' recalls Dot, fondly. 'Even at haymaking he would turn up. And then I would go and spend weekends at Ajalon. Those were lovely times because John's family made me so welcome.'

'Aye, she was the apple of my father's eye,' says John.

There was one drama which disturbed the tranquillity of their lives, when Dot was taken suddenly and seriously ill with appendicitis at her lodgings in Whitley Bay and permission to operate was urgently required from her parents.

'I got a telephone message at two o'clock one afternoon from the police saying that my fiancée was in Tynemouth Infirmary and could

I get her mother there to put her signature on this form, because they couldn't operate without it. By heck, that was the biggest dash I've ever had in my life. I got my father's car and went like a bat out of hell. There was a police escort waiting for me on the outskirts of Newcastle'.

Dot had been struck down during the night in her digs and had not been found until the following day. But she soon recovered.

At the time, John and Dot were officially engaged. On her eighteenth birthday, New Year's Day, 1956, they went to Middlesbrough and chose a ring. Dot's father pontificated a little about her being too young but both he and his wife were privately delighted at the match. There was unreserved joy at Ajalon House. John had no chance to start carving marriage spoons. By the following year they were married,

'We hadn't intended getting wed so soon but the chance of this farm came up in November, 1956. Even in those days it wasn't easy getting a farm to let — the chances were much better than today, of course, but you had no choice. There were only fifty acres but it was a case of grabbing what you could get, so I grabbed.'

The date of the wedding created the only mild friction ever to occur between Dot and John's fond father.

'He said John and I were to get married before lambing time in February, but I put my foot down and said that under no circumstances would I wear a white wedding dress in February. I decided on Easter Monday and he thought it was a ridiculous time for farming folk to marry, which I suppose was true, because it's a very busy period. Traditionally, farmers marry between sowing and harvest — round about May, just before hay making. But I was determined to choose my own wedding day whatever anyone thought.'

A good Dales wedding is a tremendous affair, particularly when it unites two well established families from the same area. It is something to plan and prepare for months, and to remember for years. The wedding of John Raw and Dorothy Welford positively resounded through the valleys of the Esk.

On the great day, each of the myriad moorland roads and winding valley lanes of East Cleveland carried at least one family heading for Glaisdale and Ajalon House to join a motley collection of vehicles which formed into a procession, headed by a hired bus. A splendid progress was then made to the bride's home at Nunthorpe and afterwards to the local parish church. The ceremony had all the trimmings, and if there was ever a truly radiant young bride then it was Dot, just nineteen. She had made her own wedding dress, complete with seventy-five buttons.

Then the feasting began. It was a home-made wedding from the dress downwards. John's father gave a ham, his mother made the cake, Dot's mother cooked and presented a traditional Dales tea, a barrel of ale was skilfully tapped and the walls of Nunthorpe

Women's Institute hall bulged with the happiness of the occasion. A group of younger male relatives slipped away to watch Middlesbrough play a match and came back to find the party still going strong. One elderly aunt was outraged because they started drinking whisky out of cups, would you believe!

The world was trembling on the brink of the Suez war at the time . . . well, that other world over the Cleveland Hills was. It would have taken something really serious, like milk fever or foot and mouth, to take the shine off that wedding. Petrol rationing meant that John could not borrow his father's car so they took the train to Edinburgh for their honeymoon, all four blissful days of it. They enjoyed it so much that they booked again—for their silver wedding. They knew even then that it would probably be that long before they would have the chance to go again. People who farm have to make sacrifices.

So John and Dot arrived, bursting with youth and hope, on the doorstep of Lawnsgate Farm, Fryup, to face—total chaos.

'I don't know how any young bride had the guts to make a start in this place,' says John, ruefully. 'For a start, it hadn't been lived in for six months. There was no running water inside, no electricity and the toilet was at the bottom of the field. There was a tap at the back, but if the farmer down below turned his tap on he took all the pressure. And it was in a real shambles. Dot had to work like a slave to get the place right but she loved it, because it was her own place. It's a good job we came when we did because we could never have brought children here as it was, or managed to afford them as we struggled to build up a farm.

'My father was very good to me—he treated all his children very well when they got married. He gave me my wages which had been accumulating over the years—seven hundred pounds, altogether. He also gave me a tractor which was only six months old, a cow, a pig, a henhouse and some tools. But we had to wait over six months before we had running water in the house. And we started the long haul to build up stock, keeping hens, growing corn, doing anything to try and better ourselves. It was a real battle trying to increase stock and affording to live, and we had some bad luck to start with. The first six years we lost a cow every year, which was a very serious matter then.'

Dot's labour of love inside the farmhouse took the best part of two years. 'I had just managed to get the place something like habitable when Shirley was born in 1958. There was still one room I hadn't touched and we still hadn't got a bathroom or indoor sanitation or electricity—we used Tilley lamps—but it wasn't bad. We had a lot of fun in those early days but what a place it was. We didn't even have fences or gates which made it difficult to stop animals straying. I remember one morning when the man came to collect the milk we were still trying to find the cow!'

106

Four months after Shirley was born, they were able to afford electricity. The following February, Susan arrived, which made John most anxious to have a son. His wish was gratified two and a half years later when Alan was born. And then came David and Christine. Five in all! As the years rolled by, John Raw's skill and expertise in farming, eight generations deep, built up a fine dairy herd and brought to Lawnsgate Farm a glory it had never known before. By his side all the time, helping him to deliver calves in the middle of the night, straining her muscles with him at haytime, lambing time and through all the crises was Dot. As their family burgeoned around them, John increased his income by securing an agency selling — from home — fertiliser and seed for a Malton farm. And their life blossomed in a way which few families are privileged to enjoy.

Lawnsgate Farm today vibrates with activity and joy as John and Dot proudly preside over the roar of five young lives, each pursuing a variety of ambitions as well as helping to run the farm.

Mark them well, for the ancient and placid rural system which produced this happy band is threatened with destruction, and we may not see their like again.

Prince

In the spring of 1973, a door was opened on the life of the Raw family for all the nation to see. For two weeks a film camera became the eighth member of the family, sitting by them, running alongside them, floating above them but never interfering with the joyous flow of the affairs of Lawnsgate Farm.

'The Children of Eskdale' came to the television screen in the purest possible form. No question was asked of the Raws, either on or off camera, and no word of commentary was spoken. Only a little music was added. Anything else would have been an unwarranted intrusion. The effect on the viewing public was profound. They were amazed at what was possible in life, that such beauty and content-ment could be achieved in the strident 'seventies. They responded to the programme in such volume, by letter, telephone and through the Press, and pleaded with such persistence to see it again at a time when children could easily watch, that it had to be repeated in the Christmas schedule of 1973.

The ease with which the Raws absorbed a camera into their daily life was never really explained. Perhaps the secret of their lifestyle lies buried there—that they are so complete as a family that nothing can disturb them. Certainly their balance was remarkable, as the documentary baton was passed effortlessly from one to the other. They appeared to cram half a year into the film, but it was an honest reflection of just two weeks of their crowded life—with one special climax.

Separately and together, there was so much life for the Raws to live. Alan, the elder son, as vital and attractive a lad as you will ever meet, was already facing up to some of the crises of life at the age of ten. There were far too many cocks in his flock of pet bantam poultry, and at least one would have to be killed and eaten. His father gently but firmly explained that if Alan was to be a farmer (should the chance arise) then he must accept that animals must come and just as surely must go. Even Gyp, their faithful farm dog, would have to be put down soon because he was sixteen. And the lesson sadly but inevitably concluded with Charlie the cock having his neck wrung.

But there were many compensations for Alan and his younger,

thoughtful brother, David — the wild fights in the haybarn, with its swings and ropes, the hilarious riding of sheep, the uninhibited chases over the hills and wild games in the old quarries; the hunting of rabbits for the stewpot with the help of the silent and sinister ferrets and the pleading for rides on the ponies of their friends.

Alongside them ran the girls, but they had their own, feminine preoccupations. Shirley, the eldest, with her father's cool appraisal of life and a motherly attitude to the mercurial junior, Christine, was concerned with her appearance. The first bra needed buying, and so did that navy-blue eye make-up which made Mother cringe. Shirley won that battle, and the one which followed over her bedroom dressing-table. Mother's probings about boyfriends and urgings about not going out of the dance hall were fenced with mocking good humour.

When Dot declared that 'you don't kiss boys — they've got germs', Shirley put back her head and pealed with laughter before suddenly shooting back: 'And what did you do when you met Dad at my age?' Which had Dot fighting to retain the initiative. But what a superb relationship it demonstrated between a mother and a daughter about to burst into womanhood.

Both Shirley and her sister Susan, who has her mother's dark hair and flashing eyes, indulge in a whirlwind of out-of-school activity which embraces amateur dramatics, ballet and tap dancing lessons, and the youth club. Add to this list the Women's Institute, the darts league, the cricket club, the quoits team and the following of the Glaisdale Hunt and there is scarcely an hour which is not filled for the Raws.

There was only one flaw in this rural idyll as far as the Raw children were concerned. They did not have their own pony. Everywhere they looked in Eskdale they saw horses, several belonging to their friends who were frequently pressed into lending them. Father Raw was subjected to a subtle and prolonged campaign, and many wide-eyed pleadings. But ponies cost serious money and there was the question of a new tractor to replace the eminently pensionable machine which had been his and Dot's principal wedding present.

'I'll buy you one if I can hunt it by day and milk it at night,' he said, as he parried adroitly.

Then one afternoon, as the young Raws wandered the lanes near Ruth Kitching's land, they were riveted by the sight of a pony pawing the ground at the top of a rolling meadow. And what a pony . . . the very stuff of which their dreams were made. A graceful Palamino called Prince with a flying blond mane, who responded to their greeting by disappearing into a hollow and then wheeling back to crest the ridge theatrically at full gallop. Five young hearts were lost forever. With many soft cooings and blandishments they entered his field and tried to tempt him near with offerings of lush grass, but he danced teasingly around them and only Alan's fingertips made

109

fleeting contact with his shining coat. From that moment on, Prince filled their thoughts and they spent wistful hours leaning over the gate to his field. It was a gallery to which Prince loved to play.

All their yearning did not pass unnoticed in this friendly Dale and it was not long before John Raw was told about his children's enslavement. He also heard that Prince might be for sale. Quietly, he went to see him . . . and realised the inevitability of the situation. John's decision was made and was ratified by Dot over coffee in the kitchen whilst the children were at school. Dot did play a somewhat unconvincing Devil's Advocate at first. 'What about the new tractor?' she asked, but she could scarcely contain her excitement at the thought of the joy it would bring to her brood.

'The tractor will have to wait. Anyway I know where I can pick up a good secondhand one. But I've made up my mind . . . and he's a beauty.'

John and Dot agreed that Prince should come as a surprise. The following evening found John in Prince's field, spitting on the palm of his hand and slapping the palm of the owner. The deal was struck . . . and John, grinning hugely at the prospect of what was to come, led Prince away down the Dale to Ruth Kitching's stables. Ruth had earlier agreed to hide Prince away for the night.

The next day dawned brightly. It was half-term holiday and Dot took the children in the car to see John's mother, leaving Dad behind to 'catch up with some work'. Prince was brought and tethered in the field at the back of Lawnsgate Farm. Then John went inside, brewed coffee and awaited the return of the children. They came in at the front of the farm, which meant that Prince was obscured from their view. The entire family sat round the table, drinking their coffee when John said: 'Alan, just nip outside for me, will you? There's a bit of bant on the back wall that I want.'

Alan dashed outside, reached for the bant — and saw Prince. The moment was unforgettable. For a split second he was paralysed, then he turned and burst into the house yelling: 'Dad . . . Dad! What's that horse doing outside?' In his excitement he had not spotted that it was Prince. John Raw managed to speak seven words — 'Well, I've bought you a horse and . . .' before the room exploded. A chair went flying as five children came out of the house like buckshot from a gun.

'It's Prince!' screamed Alan, as the realisation dawned.

'Dad, how did you know about Prince?'

The rest of the children of Eskdale were capable only of strangled noises as their pace slowed to a trance-like walk, hands outstretched towards this golden vision, as though they feared he might melt away like a mirage. Even when John picked up little Christine and gingerly placed her on Prince's back, she gurgled: 'Dad, is it really true . . .?'

'Yes, love, it *is* true,' he replied as he turned to place his arm

110

round his wife, whose eyes were brimming with tears of happiness.

And there followed such a communion of family joy, such a celebration of an enviable life that all those who were privileged to share it were swept along by its pure emotion. Many millions did share it, for two hidden cameras recorded every moment. One was built into a dry-stone wall, another shielded by bales of hay. Not for a second did the children suspect they were being filmed.

That scene became the final sequence of 'The Children of Eskdale' and it inevitably helped to release a rush of interest in the Raw family. Their mail was prodigious and scores of people sought them out. One family from the south spent an entire week's holiday trying to find them, starting in Eskdale, Scotland, progressing to Eskdale, Cumberland, before success came to them in East Cleveland on their last day. All were received with friendship, even those who stood down the lane peering at the farm through binoculars. And when the tide receded, the Raw family carried on with their lives unchanged and unchanging. As for Prince, he quickly became the best exercised pony east of the Cleveland Hills, as well as the best loved.

Making the film was a remarkable experience for the Yorkshire Television crew. They were enveloped by the warmth of the Raws and lasting relationships were forged. The children's birthdays are remembered, letters and cards sent from exotic film locations abroad and families brought to eat Dot's justly famous apple pie and curd tarts, and to stroke Prince.

Each one seemed to leave a little part of themselves behind at Lawnsgate Farm when the fortnight's location was over. During one day's filming a charge-hand electrician, a stern and senior union official, was left on his own with the Raws to rig some lighting. When the others came back he had a pitchfork in his hand and a faraway look in his eyes.

'I've fed the pigs,' he announced, 'and I'll have the mucking out done in a minute. I'd forgotten you lot existed.'

111

Postscript

It is rarely encouraging to retrace one's steps, and to go back through the valley of the Esk is no exception. During the years that followed the writing of this book the quality of life in the Yorkshire Dales has not improved, mainly due to the pressures on the agricultural system brought about by the Common Market and other largely political factors. An early warning was sounded at the end of the penultimate chapter about the Raw family — the glorious 'Children of Eskdale':

'Mark them well, for the ancient and placid system which produced this happy band is threatened with destruction, and we may not see their like again.'

The Raws have had to fight hard to hold their life together. John Raw had to take a full time job, which placed an extra burden on Dot. And it was all compounded by a series of misfortunes which sorely tried their happy state. Prince, their much loved pony, collided with a motor cycle and had to be put down — you can imagine the reaction of the children to that disaster. Then Alan, curiously, seriously injured a foot riding a motor cycle and spent a lot of time in and out of hospital as surgeons fought to save it. In recent months John had a leg crushed by a bullock and Dot has badly strained her back. On the brighter side, Shirley is now married and living in County Durham, Susan is studying for a honours degree in Sheffield and Alan, despite his handicap, is busily and cheerfully working on a farm across the dale.

Aunt Cissie, sadly, has died. At her one hundredth birthday party, when asked how she felt, she was heard to declare: 'Not too bad, but oh!—how I wish I was ninety nine again!' America Welford still rules his hillside overlooking Runswick Bay and Ruth Kitching remains totally absorbed with her stud in Fryup Dale. The clang and clamour of Scott Blowman's forge still echoes across Guisborough and enormous gooseberries flourish each summer in Egton Bridge.

But there is one over-riding shaft of pure happiness illuminating the aftermath of this book.

Mary Sunley married Jim Smith. They live in a stone-built cottage not far from Joe Sunley's farm (he, it is said, has not changed in any way) and have a baby daughter, Diane.

Barry Cockcroft
1980   112